GREAT
PREACHING

practical advice from
powerful preachers

Loveland, Colorado

Group's R.E.A.L. Guarantee® to you:

This Group resource incorporates our R.E.A.L. approach to ministry—one that encourages long-term retention and life transformation. It's ministry that's:

Relational
Because learner-to-learner interaction enhances learning and builds Christian friendships.

Experiential
Because what learners experience through discussion and action sticks with them up to 9 times longer than what they simply hear or read.

Applicable
Because the aim of Christian education is to equip learners to be both hearers and doers of God's Word.

Learner-based
Because learners understand and retain more when the learning process takes into consideration how they learn best.

Great Preaching: *Practical Advice From Powerful Preachers*
Copyright © 2003 Group Publishing, Inc.

"Preparing the Pastor's Heart for Preaching and Teaching" copyright © John Ortberg. Used by permission. "The Nature of Expository Preaching" by Alistair Begg taken from the booklet "Preaching for God's Glory." Copyright © 1999 by the Alliance of Confessing Evangelicals. Used by permission of Crossway Books, a division of Good News Publishers, Wheaton, IL 60187. "Communicating Vision by Going Public" taken from Courageous Leadership by Valerie Bell and Bill Hybels. Copyright © 2002 by Bill Hybels. Used by permission of Zondervan. "Speaking Into Crisis" copyright © Gordon MacDonald. Used by permission. "The Dynamics of Sermon Delivery" taken from *Preaching in Black and White* by Warren W. Wiersbe and E.K. Bailey. Copyright © 2003 by E.K. Bailey and Warren W. Wiersbe. Used by permission of Zondervan. "Preaching: How to Start and Stop" taken from *Preach It!* by Stuart Briscoe. Copyright © 2004 Stuart Briscoe. Used by permission of Group Publishing, Inc. "Preaching on Marriage" copyright © Bob Russell. Used by permission.

Visit our Web site: **www.grouppublishing.com**

Credits
Editor: Paul Woods
Chief Creative Officer: Joani Schultz
Copy Editor: Janis Sampson
Art Director: Sharon Anderson
Cover Art Director: Jeff A. Storm
Cover Designer: Alan Furst, Inc.
Print Production Artist: Tracy K. Hindman
Production Manager: Peggy Naylor

Unless otherwise noted, Scripture taken from the HOLY BIBLE, NEW INTERNATIONAL VERSION®. Copyright © 1973, 1978, 1984 by International Bible Society. Used by permission of Zondervan Publishing House. All rights reserved.

Library of Congress Cataloging-in-Publication Data
Great preaching : practical advice from powerful preachers.
     p. cm.
   Includes bibliographical references.
   ISBN 0-7644-2542-0 (pbk. : alk. paper)
   1. Preaching. I. Group Publishing.
BV4211.3.G74 2003
251--dc21

                                                              2003005544

10 9 8 7 6 5 4 3 2 1   12 11 10 09 08 07 06 05 04 03
Printed in the United States of America.

TABLE OF CONTENTS

INTRODUCTION

Preaching is not an easy task. It takes so much personal preparation, study, research, and practice that many pastors' weeks are nearly consumed by preaching duties. It's easy to let sermon preparation become a drudgery and allow your aspirations of being the best preacher you can be fall by the wayside. If you're like most pastors, you have to preach the sermon every weekend, ready or not. How can you avoid letting sermon preparation and presentation drag you down? How do the really great preachers do it?

Wouldn't it be great to sit down for a few hours with several great preachers and learn what they know about preaching? This book gives you that opportunity! Sixteen great preachers have shared what they believe contributes to great preaching, and *Great Preaching* tells you what they have to say.

As you'll see from the biographical sketches at the end of the chapters, these preachers come from a wide variety of Christian traditions. Each one has had years of experience in the pulpit. Some speak from a youthful perspective and others from a more seasoned outlook. Each is well-known in his own area of expertise and has put together his insights on a particular topic.

You may want to read straight through the book. Or you may decide to first read the chapters dealing with topics closest to your heart or area of need. However you choose to proceed, don't miss out on any of the great thoughts these preachers have shared in *Great Preaching!*

chapter one

PREPARING THE PASTOR'S HEART FOR PREACHING AND TEACHING

By John Ortberg

As pastors, we're devoted to a ministry of preaching and teaching. We want to do both of them well and see our churches strengthened. But how do we best prepare for this ministry? Honing communication skills isn't enough; it's also about gifting and heart preparation.

There are theological distinctions between *preaching* and *teaching*, but at Willow Creek Community Church we often let the word *teaching* cover them both. That's because the average unchurched person expects preaching to be about finger-pointing moralism, not about presenting the life-giving word of God.

So I'll use *teaching* to cover both preaching and teaching in this chapter as I share what we've discovered at Willow Creek about preparing the heart of a pastor for a teaching ministry.

It starts with a simple truth about teaching: it's important.

TEACHING IS PROFOUNDLY IMPORTANT

The Apostle Paul wrote to Timothy: "Until I come, devote yourself to the public reading of Scripture, to preaching and to teaching. Do not neglect your gift, which was given you through a prophetic message when the body of elders laid their hands on you. Be diligent in these matters; give yourself wholly to them, so that everyone may see your progress. Watch your life and doctrine closely. Persevere in them, because if you do, you will save both yourself and your hearers" (1 Timothy 4:13-16).

The verb Paul chose, *devote,* is a very strong one. It means to aim your life and to focus your private disciplines. It's a highly active command. Teaching is worthy of that kind of commitment.

At Willow Creek we focus on ten catalysts for spiritual transformation. And the number one catalyst is anointed teaching. For better or worse, teaching provides a vision for spiritual growth and motivates people to discover and use their spiritual gifts. Through teaching they learn about servanthood, and to cast the vision for community. Anointed teaching is central to evangelism and giving.

So we know two things about teaching: First, it's absolutely essential in the church. And second, we know that—at least among unchurched seekers— teaching in the church is considered outdated, irrelevant, and boring.

> gifted preachers and teachers seem to have an instinct for finding a way to communicate.

Here's the question then: How do you make sure there's timely, relevant, and engaging teaching in your church—especially if *you're* the teacher?

MAKE SURE YOU HAVE THE SPIRITUAL GIFT OF TEACHING

In 1 Corinthians 12:20, Paul writes that there are many parts of the body, but just one body. As part of the body, we are gifted in some areas but not in others. We can't do everything well, which means we don't all teach well. There are people who simply aren't gifted to teach.

When I was in seminary, I took classes about teaching. I practiced teaching and was coached about how to improve. But at no time did anyone ever ask me if I had the spiritual gift of teaching.

Perhaps that was your experience too. How *do* you determine if you're the right person to be teaching in your church? The question is not "Am I skilled?" or "Am I capable?" but "Am I *gifted?*"

PREPARING THE PASTOR'S HEART

I'm particularly indebted to Bill Hybels for some thoughts on this subject. I'd like to lay out six indicators and encourage you to rate yourself. Do you have a high resonance with each indicator? Does it show in your life? Or is it only occasionally true of you or typically not true at all?

■ 1. People with a gift of teaching tend to enjoy the process of preparing a message.

People with a gift in this area look forward to preparing messages. They enjoy studying God's Word.

In one sense this is fairly normal. Most Christians enjoy devotional study. But gifted teachers go further. They enjoy studying the context of a passage and finding out about the background and history that sheds light on what they're reading. They often study biblical languages or at least learn exegetical information about passages. They delve into commentaries and theology and doctrine. All of this is *not* normal for the average person.

Gifted teachers enjoy diving deeply into God's Word.

■ 2. People with a gift of teaching tend to experience both illumination and communication when they study Scripture.

Gifted teachers not only understand what's being said in a text—that's the illumination—but they also understand how to communicate that information to other people. These teachers actively seek to make biblical truth accessible and compelling to others. They're always looking for ways to make Bible content come alive. It's like a little motor that's always running in their heads.

Gifted preachers and teachers seem to have an instinct for finding a way to communicate. They zero in on one key point, the single most penetrating part of a Bible narrative.

■ 3. People with a gift of teaching live with the absolute conviction that God's Word can transform lives.

There's a spiritual battle going on, and teachers enter into that battle. As a general rule, gifted teachers are gripped with the conviction that the Word of God is able to transform lives. Gifted teachers believe the Word of God contains wisdom, and the human race desperately needs wisdom.

■ 4. People with a gift of teaching tend to have a God-given ability to read and respond to a congregation.

These teachers can sense the attitude and spiritual receptivity of people they're teaching. When you find this trait in one-on-one relationships, psychologists use the word *attunement* to describe it. A partner who's attuned to you can read your body language and pick up on subtle signs that you're listening, bored, or have something to say.

People with a gift of teaching are able to do that with an entire congregation.

Gifted teachers can sense when attention is wandering or when humor is appropriate—or inappropriate. They can discern when people are receptive to a challenge. They can read moments and respond to them because there's a connection between them and their audience.

> For highly gifted teachers, connecting with an audience is a joyful emotional experience.

For highly gifted teachers, connecting with an audience is a joyful emotional experience. Failing to connect is intensely painful. These are teachers who passionately believe that what they have to share is of great value, so they want to reach every person in the room.

■ 5. People with a gift of teaching tend to receive widespread affirmation for their teaching.

This doesn't just mean they hear the obligatory, "Nice job, Pastor," as people file out after the service. That doesn't count for much because some people would say that even if you stood up and read out of the phone book.

I'm talking about hearing comments that indicate that lives are changing. That people are being saved. That people are repenting of sin. That people who are separated from each other reconcile. That people whose marriages are spiraling downward get on the road to healing. That people who are selfish and greedy begin to give. That people who are self-centered get inspired to serve.

People who have a gift of teaching and who use that gift in a spirit of servanthood under the anointing of the Holy Spirit see an impact and are affirmed for their teaching. God uses them regularly to share messages that change lives.

■ *6. People with a gift of teaching often feel a quiet assurance of the Holy Spirit that they're in the right roles for the right reasons.*

People who are gifted in this area feel that this is what they were made to do. It's who they are. When they're teaching, they're most fully alive.

A teacher who's had a huge impact on my life is Dallas Willard. I was talking with him once and asked what it was that most bolsters his faith and belief in God. The first thing Dallas said was this: "It's the disproportionate impact of what I say on people's lives."

Isn't that great? Because he's a gifted teacher, God uses his words to bring about life-change far beyond anything that Dallas could cause himself.

If you went through this exercise and discovered that none of these indicators sound like you, I have three words for you: God loves you.

He does. Don't doubt it. But you may have fallen prey to one of the myths of our society: You can do or be anything you want to be. Scripture is clear that you *can't* do or be anything you want to be. We all have areas of giftedness and areas in which we aren't gifted. We don't get to choose. It may be that teaching isn't at the top of your gift mix, but comes in second, third, or fourth. Fine—teach, but not every week. There's something else you should be doing in a primary way.

If it's not in your gift mix at all, be honest and say so. Life is too short to be in the wrong place. Your life matters too much, and the church matters too much, for you to be serving in an area in which you don't have gifts.

| IMPROVE YOUR EFFECTIVENESS AS A TEACHER | Let's say you have a gift to teach. Some of the above indicators do apply to you. Your heart's in it. You're a willing servant. How can you improve in your effectiveness? Here are a few suggestions. |

■ *1. Listen to good teaching.*

Listen to tapes and people on the radio, watch teachers on videos or television, and sit under great teachers in person.

Discern why these teachers are effective. The goal isn't to mimic these folks but to learn from them.

Brainstorm with other teachers. Be teachable and willing to grow.

■ 2. Understand what's at stake in a teaching ministry.

If I'm not careful, my focus can become "How well am I teaching?" I zero in on myself and my abilities and not on the power of God's Word. The purpose of teaching is to let people know who God is and how to respond to God. It's not about me.

When I've centered on being helpful and not worried about how well I'm doing, I've done all right. When I've shifted my eyes to "How am I doing?" that's when I've gotten in trouble.

■ 3. Cultivate a deep, rich, inner life with Christ.

Is the life you're inviting others to live, the life you're living yourself? If I'm going to teach others to have a deep, growing relationship with God, I need one too. For me that means embracing some spiritual disciplines that connect me with God and help me receive power to overcome problems.

Here are four disciplines I believe we as teachers need to practice.

• **Solitude:** Solitude is good for teachers, in part because the primary characteristic of solitude isn't what you do—it's what you *don't* do. You withdraw from the scaffolding of your life—no meetings, no noise, no stimulation, no lessons to prepare. It's just you and God.

> At least once a month, I schedule a half-day to be in solitude.

As teachers leading public lives, we begin to think we're only as good as our last sermon series. In solitude alone with God, we have the opportunity to remember we aren't who people tell us we are. We're who God tells us we are.

At least once a month, I schedule a half-day to be in solitude.

• **Silence:** The early church fathers frequently recommended that believers practice silence. And the top reason they endorsed silence is that it's difficult to talk without sinning.

The average person lies—a lot. I wish I was immune to that temptation, but I'm not. At Willow Creek we're constantly encouraging people to grow, constantly motivating people to engage and change. I find that if I use that gear too much, I begin casting a vision that I don't really have. It's hype—and being in "hype mode" is very spiritually destructive.

But to sit and be still...to be *silent*...that makes me aware of my words when I do speak.

• **Confession:** Because we teachers tend to project what we want people to see, it's healthy to let at least one person know everything there is to know about you.

> secrets are dangerous—especially in the lives of us teachers.

The first time I was totally open with someone, I chose a friend I'd known for ten years. Even with our high level of trust, it was difficult for me. For an hour and a half I walked Rick through things I didn't want anyone to know. When I finished, Rick said, "John, I love you more now than I've ever loved you during our entire friendship."

James 5:16 says to confess our sins one to another. There's power there. Secrets are dangerous—especially in the lives of us teachers.

But here's the truth: We have to *decide* to be accountable. Nobody can impose accountability on you. If you really want to avoid it, you can. Don't.

• **Secrecy—the good kind:** In Matthew 6, Jesus says to be careful about doing acts of righteousness in order to be seen by men. Jesus isn't suggesting you can never tell anyone you're fasting. Rather, he's addressing a spiritual condition found in some people. We want to do good deeds, but we want to get credit for them.

Instead, Jesus says to do good without looking for applause. Doing good stuff without recognition reminds you that you serve because it pleases God, not because it impresses people.

■ 4. Be clear on what you want to accomplish.

In Mark 1:14-15, Mark summarizes what Jesus did during his ministry: "After John was put in prison, Jesus went into Galilee, proclaiming the good news of God. 'The time has come,' he said. 'The kingdom of God is near. Repent and believe the good news!' "

Jesus' ministry was primarily a *teaching* ministry. He proclaimed God's story, then called people to repent and trust. Jesus wanted to transform lives, not just transfer information. Jesus kept it simple: Know God. Respond to God.

FOCUS ON THE CORE VALUES OF LIFE-CHANGING TEACHING

Our teaching can transform lives too. At Willow Creek we've worked hard to identify core values of life-changing teaching. Here's what we've found:

Life-changing teaching is biblical.

You and I don't change lives; God's Word changes lives. Teaching must be biblical to be effective.

But what makes a message biblical? It's not that you teach through a passage verse by verse. That wasn't the approach Jesus used. Usually he told stories. Biblical teaching has less to do with technique and more to do with focus. When listeners are able to see how their world is addressed by the Word of God and empowered to respond, *that's* biblical teaching. Too many sermons are loaded with information about the Bible, but there's never a call to respond.

Life-changing teaching is purposeful.

I always ask three questions when I'm preparing a message:

* ***What do I want people to understand?*** This gets at what truth I want people to experience. How will I engage their intellect?

* ***What do I want people to feel?*** How will I engage people emotionally? How do I want them to feel about God or the church?

* ***What do I want people to do?*** What decision am I calling people to make? What action do I want to see as people apply the Bible truth I've shared?

If you can't answer those questions when it's time to deliver your next message, then don't deliver it at all. You're not ready.

Life-changing teaching is urgent.

Life-changing teaching comes out of a passionate belief in the power of God's Word proclaimed. Teaching that's devoid of passion is just a series of interesting ideas.

So what do you do if you're not feeling passion? if you're weary? if the text you're teaching from just doesn't prompt passion in you?

Some suggestions…

• ***Don't fake it.*** Shouting louder doesn't make you passionate, it makes you louder. People can smell faked passion—and it isn't fragrant.

• ***Think of why some people who'll be listening need to hear this message.*** Never teach to a faceless crowd; think of specific people who need to hear what you're sharing. Keep them in mind as you prepare your message.

• ***Ask God to fuel your passion.*** What good things will happen if people understand what God's Word says about your topic? Ask God to show you.

• ***Ask yourself: Am I speaking too much?*** You're capable of just so much sustained passion. You're probably like me: I can gear up and speak passionately just so often. If I'm trying to prepare too many messages or speak at too many services, I begin to fade.

And if you feel no passion for a subject and can't think of why anyone else would feel passion for it, perhaps you're teaching about the wrong subject. You have a limited amount of opportunities to teach; don't use them speaking about the wrong things.

Life-changing teaching is balanced.

Don't fall into the trap of teaching only about your favorite subjects and passages. You need balance. You need balance between speaking to your audiences' hearts and their heads. Between comforting and challenging. Between what's familiar and what's unfamiliar. Between Old and New Testaments.

Your church needs to study the *whole* counsel of God, not just your pet passages. It's *all* inspired of God. Balance what portions of Scripture you teach.

Life-changing teaching is authentic.

People don't trust teachers who are unwilling to reveal their own humanity. Appropriate self-disclosure is one of a teacher's most powerful tools.

Here's a rule of thumb for making sure self-disclosure is appropriate: Share what people need to hear, not what you need to talk about. The platform isn't a place for self-therapy or venting. Will what you share from your own life facilitate the message or get in the way?

And two tips to tuck away:

* *When it comes to sharing about your family, be very careful.* Share only those stories you've cleared beforehand.

* *Moments in your church life that are unresolved or awkward are often great opportunities for teaching.* In most churches, unresolved issues never are identified and dealt with openly.

Life-changing teaching is creative.

People's ability to give sustained attention is growing weaker and weaker. That means as teachers we have to grow ever more creative. Involve the senses. Involve people. Use video, art, props, drama, activities, and discussions. Even low-tech flip charts have an impact. There's something about picking up a pen and walking over to a flip chart that causes people to quiet down and pay attention as you start to write.

Life-changing teaching involves a strong work ethic.

Push yourself. Determine that you won't go into a service to teach until you can say, "This is the best I can do."

Be willing to do the work. To call someone if you're stuck. To put in the study time necessary. To get feedback. Commit before God you'll get the message in excellent shape—*before* you teach.

Some teachers, especially glib ones, are tempted to think, "I'll just get up there and see if something good happens." Don't do it.

Your ministry of teaching is just too important to take lightly. It's not a task to cross off. It's a God-given opportunity and responsibility.

You're using a gift. Proclaiming the gospel. Shining light into darkness. It's worthy of your best preparation.

This chapter is derived from "Leadership Summit Preaching That Changes Lives" audiotapes.

John Ortberg is a teaching pastor at Willow Creek Community Church in South Barrington, Illinois. Each week he speaks to thousands of people at the church's New Community services. John is the author of several books, including *If You Want to Walk on Water, You've Got to Get Out of the Boat; The Life You've Always Wanted;* and *Love Beyond Reason.* John has also written for Christianity Today and is a frequent contributor to Leadership Journal.

chapter two

THE NATURE OF EXPOSITORY PREACHING

By Alistair Begg

No treatment of the nature of expository preaching would be complete without referring to the dramatic scene recorded in Nehemiah 8:

> All the people assembled as one man in the square before the water gate. They told Ezra the scribe to bring out the Book of the Law of Moses, which the Lord had commanded for Israel...He read it aloud from daybreak till noon as he faced the square before the water gate in the presence of the men, women and others who could understand. And all the people listened attentively to the Book of the Law...The Levites...instructed the people in the Law while the people were standing there. They read from the Book of the Law of God, making it clear and giving the meaning so that the people could understand what was being read (Nehemiah 8:1, 3, 7-8).

The sense of expectation among those people was almost palpable. Can it be wrong for us to long for our people to gather to wait upon the preaching of the Word with the same passion and hunger?

Such a heightened sense of expectation is inevitably tied to a high view of Scripture. There's a dramatic difference between the congregation that gathers in anticipation of a monologue on biblical matters from a kindly fellow and the one that has come expecting that when God's Word is truly preached, God's voice is really heard. Calvin expresses this in his commentary on Ephesians: "It is certain that if we come to church we shall not hear only a mortal man speaking but we shall feel (even by his secret power) that God is speaking to our souls, that he is the teacher. He so touches us that the human voice enters into us and so profits us that we are refreshed and nourished by it. God calls us to him as if he had his mouth open and we saw him there in person."[1]

> what are the key principles of expository preaching?

On one occasion a visitor to Gilcomston South Church in Aberdeen, while greeting the minister, William Still, at the conclusion of a sermon, commented, "But you don't preach." When the pastor asked what he meant, the man answered, "You just take a passage from the Bible and explain what it means." Mr. Still replied, "Brother, that is preaching!"

He and others like him are simply following the pattern for expository preaching established by Ezra and his colleagues. Those godly men read God's Book and explained it, and they did so in such a way that people understood the implications.

How are we to accomplish this? What are the key principles of expository preaching?

BEGIN WITH THE TEXT

Expository preaching always begins with the text of Scripture.

That does not mean every sermon will begin with the phrase, "Please turn in your Bible to…" But it does mean that even when we begin by referring to some current event or the lyric of a contemporary song, it's the text of Scripture that establishes the agenda for the sermon. The Bible expositor doesn't start with an idea or a great illustration and then search for an appropriate passage. Instead he begins with the Scripture itself and allows the verses under consideration to establish and frame the content of the sermon. This is why, as John Stott

THE NATURE OF EXPOSITORY PR

says, "It is our conviction that all true Christian preaching is expository preaching."[2] We are on the wrong track if we think of expository preaching merely as a preaching *style* chosen from a list (topical, devotional, evangelistic, textual, apologetic, prophetic, expository).

Roy Clements says rightly, "Expository preaching is not a matter of style at all. In fact, the determinative step which decides whether a sermon is going to be expository or not takes place, in my view, before a single word has been actually written or spoken. First and foremost, the adjective *expository* describes the method by which the preacher decides what to say, not how to say it."[3]

Exposition is not simply a running commentary on a passage of Scripture. Nor is it a succession of word studies held loosely together by a few illustrations. We should not even think of it in terms of the discovery and declaration of the central doctrine found in the passage. We can do all that without accomplishing biblical exposition in terms of the definition we're building.

| STAND BETWEEN TWO WORLDS | *Expository preaching seeks to fuse the two horizons of the biblical text and the contemporary world.* This insight is worked out thoroughly by John Stott in *Between Two Worlds: The Art of Preaching in the* |

Twentieth Century. Stott argues rightly that it's possible to preach exegetically and yet fail to answer the "so what?" in the listener's mind. Ezra's hearers, for example, would never have begun construction of the booths if he had failed to establish the link between the text and the times. True exposition must have some prophetic dimension that leaves the listener in no doubt that what he has heard is a living word from God and creates in him at least the sneaking suspicion that the Author knows him.

If we're going to take the challenge to teach the Bible in this way seriously, we must pay attention to the warning of a twentieth-century Scottish preacher who said that it's sheer slackness to fling at people great slabs of religious phraseology derived from the bygone age without helping them retranslate the message into their own experience. That's the preacher's task, not theirs, he argued.

The rediscovery of the theological works of the Puritans is something for which we're all grateful; but at the same time the proliferation of young men whose pulpit delivery owes more to the seventeenth century than to the twenty-first should be a cause for concern. Of course, the problem is arguably far more significant at the other end of the spectrum, where we find sermons that are overly steeped in the issues and interests of contemporary culture. Such preaching tends to establish contact with the listener very quickly, but its connection with the Bible is so slight that it fails to establish the link between the world of the Bible and the personal world of the listener. The preacher's task is to declare what God has said, explain the meaning, and establish the implications so that no one will mistake its relevance.

Donald Grey Barnhouse frequently described this task as "the art of explaining the text of the Word of God, using all the experience of life and learning to illuminate the exposition."

Expository preaching encourages the listener to understand why a first-century letter to the church in Corinth is relevant to a twenty-first-century congregation living in Cleveland.

It's important that the listener doesn't leave mystified by the way in which the preacher dealt with the text. The preacher must learn not simply to fuse the horizons in his teaching, but to do so in such a way that the people are learning by example how to integrate the Bible with their own experience. Listeners face the twin dangers of assuming either that what they have just heard is totally unrelated to where they're living or that it's *immediately* applicable, that it's "just for them." Allow me to explain further about these two dangers.

■ *1. That the message is irrelevant.*

The preacher must work hard to ensure that he hasn't simply done good exegesis, helping the listener to understand the meaning of the text, but has also labored to establish its relevance to the listener's personal world. For example, in addressing the doctrine of the incarnation, he must not content himself with simply ensuring that his listeners have grasped the instruction but will point out the implications of the great principle of "incarnational mission." To establish that link the preacher may say something along the lines of, "The ministry of Jesus was one of involvement, not detachment; and therefore we must face the fact that we can't minister to a lost world if we're not in it."

■ *2. That the message is immediately relevant.*

The second danger is just as real. Here the listener wants to move immediately to application. He'll be anxious to know "what this means to *me*." In many cases this rush to personalize the text will be removed from the necessary understanding of what the passage means in its original context.

I know of no one who has been more helpful in getting preachers to wrestle with this than Dick Lucas. Those of us who in presenting our work to a jury of our peers have been brought to an abrupt halt by Dick's, "Come now, dear boy, that's surely not what the apostle means!" will not soon forget the experience. I'm very grateful that he has made me wary of trying to apply the text to Cleveland before I've discovered Paul's purpose in addressing the congregation in first-century Corinth.

> "come now, dear boy, that's surely not what the apostle means!"

It's clearly possible, for example, to unearth a text like Hebrews 13:8 ("Jesus Christ is the same yesterday and today and forever") from the surrounding context and do an adequate job of speaking about the benefits to the believer of a Jesus who is unchanging. But if we want our listeners to learn how to interpret the Bible, we must do the hard work of understanding why verse 8 appears between verses 7 and 9. If we do that work, we'll find it necessary to explain our verse not simply in isolation or in terms of our immediate context but in the wider context of the book. We'll recognize that any application that does not focus on the permanent priesthood of Christ will not only have missed the point but will have done a disservice to our people who are learning with us.

The expositor needs to be under the control of Scripture. This is the third of three principles for faithful exposition provided by the *Westminster Directory for Public Worship*:

■ *1. The matter we preach should be true; that is, in the light of general doctrines of Scripture.*

■ *2. It should be the truth contained in the text or passage we are expounding.*

■ *3. It should be the truth preached under the control of the rest of Scripture.*

What a radical change would come about in pulpits all across the country if we were to take these three principles seriously. We would be forced to ensure that the pulpit did not afford a place for theorizing and speculation, for sloganeering and manipulation, for tall stories and emotionalism. In an earlier era in Scotland when great pains were taken to abide by these principles, the impact was obvious. Indeed, the knowledge of the Bible possessed by our ordinary congregations, amid all our supposed understanding and enlightenment, bears no comparison with that of simple Scottish people of the last generation who were taught from infancy to follow the preacher's teaching from the Bible. Although that was long before my time, the benefit lingered, and I can still recall my father's slightly trembling hand as it held the Bible and his finger guided my gaze along the page. How magnificent it is when God ministers to our hearts through the power of expository preaching!

THE BENEFITS OF EXPOSITORY PREACHING

There are immense benefits of expository preaching that are not present to the same degree, if at all, in other types of preaching. These alone are compelling arguments as to why genuine expository preaching should be recovered and faithfully practiced in our day. We'll now review these benefits.

IT GIVES
GLORY TO
GOD ALONE

Expository preaching gives glory to God, which ought to be the ultimate end of all we do.

The psalmist declares, "You have exalted above all things your name and your word" (Psalm 138:2b). Since expository preaching begins with the text of Scripture, it starts with God and is in itself an act of worship, for it is a declaration of the mighty acts of God. It establishes the focus of the people upon God and his glory before any consideration of man and his need. In beginning here we affirm the place of preaching not on the grounds of personal interest but because it pleases God. A congregation that has accepted this and is beginning to learn the implications of it will be markedly different from one in which sermons constantly find their origin in the felt needs of the people.

IT MAKES THE PREACHER STUDY GOD'S WORD	*Expository preaching demands that the preacher himself become a student of the Word of God.*

After seminary, serving in their first church, pastors study to produce a variety of sermons. But some, having preached them all, then move on to give another congregation the benefit of their study. By contrast when a pastor is committed to the systematic and consecutive exposition of Scripture, he will never come to an end of his task. If we are not learning, we are not growing; and if we are stuck, we can be certain that our people will be stuck with us. It is vital that we keep coming to the Scriptures in the spirit of discovery. We must learn to look for the surprises in the passage. We should not assume that we "understand" just because we have spent time in this passage before. Rather, we should always be praying:

> *O teach me, Lord, that I may teach*
> *The precious things Thou dost impart;*
> *And wing my words that they may reach*
> *The hidden depths of many a heart.*

The first heart God's Word needs to reach is that of the preacher. There will be no benefit to our people from expository preaching unless we ourselves are being impacted by the Scripture we're preparing to preach. It's imperative, when we're dealing with the biblical text, that we're personally changed by it. John Owen spoke of this necessity of experiencing the power of truth in our own souls: "A man only preaches a sermon well to others if he has first preached it to himself. If he does not thrive on the 'food' he prepares, he will not be skilled at making it appetizing for others. If the Word does not dwell in power in us, it will not pass in power from us."[4]

IT HELPS THE CONGREGATION	*Expository preaching enables the congregation to learn the Bible in the most obvious and natural way.*

We would not expect a university professor to teach from a textbook on the human anatomy by picking out parts of sentences at random and using them for his lecture. Rather, we would anticipate his working through the material in an orderly fashion to ensure that his students come to understand how the pieces fit together.

Many men are capable of delivering excellent orations, producing touching illustrations, and uttering stirring exhortations based on scriptural material but as expositors of Scripture are ineffective. Spurgeon in lectures to his students observed, "If you attend to a lecturer on astronomy or geology, during a short course you will obtain a tolerably clear view of his system; but if you listen...for twelve years, to the common run of preachers, you will not arrive at anything like an idea of their system of theology."[5]

By our preaching we either help or hinder our people in the task of interpreting Scripture. If we merely show them the results of our study without at least to some degree including them in the process, they may be "blessed" but will remain untaught. To borrow again from Roy Clements, "It is no longer enough to feed our people. These days we must also show them how to cook."

IT DEMANDS TREATMENT OF THE ENTIRE BIBLE

Expository preaching prevents the preacher from avoiding difficult passages or from dwelling on his favorite texts.

This is no small matter. The computer on which I'm presently working has a screen saver. Whenever there has been an absence of activity for any significant length of time, it automatically defaults to one particular image. In a similar fashion, when the preacher has not been active in the systematic study of Scripture, he will find himself defaulting to his pet passages to save face. For some this might be "higher life" teaching or an emphasis on "the risen life of Christ." Others default to flights of eschatological fancy that are guaranteed to intrigue but that seldom manage to instruct. Whatever the emphasis may be, it will in time become an overemphasis, and the congregation will come to expect only that for which the preacher has become known.

By this methodology many congregations are denied the opportunity to wrestle with the mind-stretching, soul-stirring doctrine of election. Others have never examined the issue of spiritual gifts or have managed to avoid consideration of "controversial" subjects like homosexuality, the role of women, or the future of Israel. By committing himself to an exposition of the Scripture that is systematic in its pattern, the preacher will avoid these pitfalls.

Expository preaching assures the congregation of enjoying a balanced diet of God's Word.

This is the reverse of the previous point. Each of us comes to a given text of Scripture with a framework. It may be something as simple as the slogan "The Old (Testament) is in the New revealed; the New is in the Old concealed." Or it may be, "We find Christ in all the Scriptures. In the Old Testament he is predicted, in the Gospels he is revealed, in the Acts he is preached, in the epistles he is explained, and in the Revelation he is expected." We use such frameworks to help us navigate the Scriptures. Certainly they have value.

However, there's a danger when the framework is more substantial than in the illustrations above. In such a case, instead of the text of Scripture dictating to our framework, whether it's a dispensational or covenant hermeneutic or whatever, we allow the tail to wag the dog.

Also, sometimes the framework is the product of a denominational distinctive that creates an imbalance. For example, I was worshipping in a church in South Carolina where the pastor was doing a series of studies from 1 Timothy. The passage for that morning was the first thirteen verses of the third chapter. In opening up the text he said something like this: "The first seven verses have to do with elders, but since we are Baptists we don't have them. So let's go directly to verse 8, which deals with deacons!"

Expository preaching need not be limited to exhaustive and exhausting studies through books of the Bible.

On another occasion I was worshipping in Grand Rapids, Michigan. The pastor was dealing with the subject of Communion, and I quickly lost track of how many times he urged us to consult the copy of the Heidelberg Catechism sitting before us in the pews. One might have been forgiven for wondering whether the ultimate authority was the Bible or the catechism.

Exposition, which constantly affirms the priority and sufficiency of the text, will prevent such an imbalance from taking place. As a result we risk being regarded as being less than precise on our systematic theology; but we should not be more precise than the text of Scripture allows.

Teaching the Bible in this way should not mean a lack of variety. In fact, the variety inherent in the Bible itself should be present in our preaching. Expository preaching need not be limited to exhaustive and exhausting studies through books of the Bible. Ninety percent of what I do is careful study of particular Bible books, but we can also do character studies or a series on the parables in Luke or on key Christian doctrines and tackle each of them in an expository form. For example, in preaching on the matter of temptation, we can expound the first half of James 1 rather than pulling together material from all over the Bible. We serve our people best when we make clear that we're committed to teaching the Bible *by teaching the Bible!*

| IT ELIMINATES SATURDAY NIGHT FEVER | *Expository preaching liberates the preacher from the pressure of last-minute preparation on Saturday night.* |

Expository preaching liberates the preacher from the pressure of last-minute preparation on Saturday night.

Expository preaching that's systematic and consecutive in its pattern means that the congregation doesn't approach church asking themselves, "I wonder what the minister will preach about today?" And the pastor is freed from facing the same question with painful, relentless regularity. From a pragmatic perspective, that alone is enough to convince me of the value of expository preaching.

Following the example of my mentor, Derek Prime, I often take a break in the middle of a long series, perhaps on 1 Corinthians or John's Gospel, by doing a mini-series on something else. This gives the preacher and the people a purposeful pause and allows both to return to the main series with fresh expectation. On a very limited number of occasions, I've also interrupted a series in order to address a subject that has gripped the congregation or the nation. But this is different from the all too familiar picture of the pastor in his study on a Saturday evening with his hair disheveled, surrounded by balls of paper, each of which represents a sermon idea that refused to be born. Even the great Spurgeon was often perilously close to this danger. He acknowledged: "I confess that I frequently sit hour after hour praying and waiting for a subject...I believe that almost any Saturday in my life I make enough outlines of sermons, if I felt the liberty to preach them, to last me for a month."[6]

But Spurgeon was unique, perhaps even a genius. Shall we allow his pattern to overturn the points I have labored to make? I think not. All we need to acknowledge is that God does not come upon methods but upon men, even when our methods may not give the appearance of being the wisest or the best. I have often imagined how grand it would be to be able to turn to volumes of Spurgeon's consecutive exposition rather than the collections of sermons he has actually left to us, as

> The best of men are men at best. There has only ever been one perfect preacher, and that is Jesus.

rich as they are. Spurgeon serves as a reminder that the best of men are men at best and that there has only ever been one perfect preacher, and that is Jesus.

PRACTICAL POINTERS

I've always been fascinated by the variety of approaches that preachers take in preparing their sermons. In our delivery and in our preparation, we must "to our own selves be true." Some have a unique facility of memory; others are expert in the use of technology. Some of us are still working with legal pads and pencils. Probably the only factor that we all share is that we come to the text upon our knees, at least figuratively. The attitude of heart with which we come to our preparation should express our dependence upon God.

Whenever I am asked to summarize my own method of preparation, I mention the following points, which I learned from an older minister when I was still a theological student.

THINK YOURSELF EMPTY It's helpful if we can survey the passage in a proper spirit of unlearnedness. We don't want to be uncertain by the time our study ends, but it's all right and often beneficial to avoid the proud assumption that we know initially what everything means. Obviously as time passes, we'll have a greater grasp of more and more material, but it's always good to train our minds to expect the unexpected. This will open up new avenues of thought and create angles of approach that we may never have seen before. In this stage I write down anything that comes to mind—parallel passages, possible illustrations, textual difficulties, poems, hymn quotes, a sketchy outline if it emerges naturally. Much of what goes on that initial page will never become part of the sermon, but that doesn't matter. The humbling part of this is when it takes only five minutes to think ourselves empty and there's very little to show for it on the largely empty page!

The point is, if we don't become thinking pastors, we're unlikely to have thinking congregations.

READ YOURSELF FULL

The pastor should read widely and regularly. There are certain books we should return to routinely: Baxter's *The Reformed Pastor,* Augustine's *Confessions,* and, as daunting as we may find it, Calvin's *Institutes.* I also find great profit in reading biographies. The two volumes on Lloyd-Jones should be a prerequisite for all pastors, as well as at least the first volume on Whitefield by Arnold Dallimore. There's also profit in the biographies of politicians, musicians, golfers, and various others. (I betray here my personal interests.) Novels that pass the Philippians 4:8 test are also helpful. Along with this I personally am helped by book reviews in The New York Times, and even the obituaries. As time allows, it's also important to read material from competing perspectives. This helps us sharpen our wits and keeps us on our theological toes.

In reading about the text from which we're about to preach, there are many useful resources: *The New International Commentary* on both the Old and New Testaments, Lenski on the New Testament, the Hendriksen commentary series, and many more. We must learn to benefit from these resources without becoming tied to them or allowing their insights to rob us of the necessary personal experience of discovery and creativity.

WRITE YOURSELF CLEAR

Aside from the essential empowering of the Holy Spirit, if there's one single aspect of sermon preparation that's most closely tied to fluency of speech and impact in its delivery, it's this: Freedom of delivery in the pulpit depends upon careful organization in the study. We may believe that we have a grasp of the text and that we're clear about our delivery, only to stand up and discover that somewhere between our thinking and our speaking things have gone badly awry. The missing link can usually be traced to the absence of putting our thoughts down clearly.

James S. Stewart tells the story of a young minister who, concerned about the apparent failure of his preaching, consulted Dr. Joseph Parker in the vestry of the City Temple. His sermons, he complained, were producing only apathy. Could Dr. Parker frankly tell him what was lacking? "Suppose you preach me one of your sermons now," said Parker. His visitor, not without some trepidation, complied. When it was over, Parker told him to

> Freedom of delivery in the pulpit depends upon careful organization in the study.

sit down. "Young man," he said, "you asked me to be frank. I think I can tell you what is the matter. For the last half-hour you have been trying to get something out of your head instead of something into mine!"

When we take the time to commit not only our thoughts but our sentences and paragraphs and linking phrases to paper, we'll quickly detect the *non sequiturs* and be able to make corrections long before we're presenting the material in a public forum. When a speaker gives the impression that he's working out what he's trying to say as he's speaking, he probably is!

In most cases both the speaker and the listeners will be helped by some kind of outline, and this generally emerges in the writing stage, if not before. But the preacher and the congregation should both only be helped to think clearly, not overpowered by the cleverness or weight of the outline. Eric Alexander observes, "The structure must never obtrude so as to be admired for its cleverness or originality. It needs to represent the content of the passage...It is the finished building men want to see and not the builder's scaffolding."[7]

PRAY YOURSELF HOT

There's no chance of fire in the pews if there's an iceberg in the pulpit; and without personal prayer and communion with God during the preparation stages, the pulpit will be cold. When the apostles did some reorganization of the early church, it was because they realized how crucial it was for them to give themselves continually to "prayer and the ministry of the word" (Acts 6:4). To borrow from the marriage ceremony, it's imperative that "what God has joined together, no man should put asunder." We dare not divorce our preaching from our praying.

In an ordination sermon preached in Bridgewater, Massachusetts, in 1752, John Shaw reminded the incumbent pastor: "If any men in the world need the special presence of God with them, and his blessing in order to succeed, certainly ministers do...God looks for their prayers to come up to his ears. A praying minister is in the way to have a successful ministry."[8]

We can do more than pray, after we have prayed, but not until. How easy it is to affirm this, and yet how difficult to practice.

There's nothing quite so ridiculous as the affected tone and adopted posture of the preacher who wishes he were someone else. Sadly, it's common to listen to someone preach, recognize the tone of voice and the style of delivery, and know that it doesn't conform to the individual who's preaching. While we can and must learn from those whom God has used to great effect in the pulpit, our admiration dare not lead to imitation.

James Stewart used to say, "Be yourself, but also, forget yourself!" Self-forgetfulness is of vital importance. We can't make much of ourselves and much of the Lord Jesus Christ simultaneously. If people leave worship saying, "What an amazing preacher!" we've failed. Instead we must long for them to say, " What a great God, and what a privilege it is to meet him in his Word, as we have just done." A good teacher clears the way, declares the way, and then gets out of the way.

We dare not miss the seriousness of this. Three hundred years ago, Richard Baxter chided pastors he knew for behaving so "weakly, unhandsomely, imprudently and so slightly" when they were entrusted by God with delivering a message of eternal consequences to the souls of men. We must be warned of this, too, and never more so than when we are guilty of pretense. If God has made us a piccolo, we should be content to play our part; if a tuba, then let us strike those low notes with authority. But let not the cello seek to imitate or envy the French horn. We must play the notes prepared for us...and always in the key of *B natural!*

> A good teacher clears the way, declares the way, and then gets out of the way.

May God bless each of us as we seek to serve him and our congregations through expository preaching—preaching done in his way for his glory!

NOTES

1. John Calvin, *Ephesians* (Edinburgh and Carlisle, PA: Banner of Truth, 1973), 42.

2. John Stott, *Between Two Worlds* (Grand Rapids, MI: Wm. B. Eerdmans Publishing Company, 1982), 125.

3. Roy Clements, *The Cambridge Papers,* September 1998.

4. John Owen, *The Works of John Owen,* Vol. 16 (Edinburgh and Carlisle, PA: Banner of Truth, 1968), 76.

5. C.H. Spurgeon, *Lectures to My Students* (Grand Rapids, MI: Zondervan, 1972), 71.

6. C.H. Spurgeon, *Lectures to My Students,* 84-85.

7. Eric Alexander, "Plainly Teaching the Word," unpublished message delivered to the Toronto Spiritual Life Conference, January 10, 1989.

8. John Shaw, *The Character of a Pastor According to God's Heart Considered* (Morgan, PA: Soli Deo Gloria, 1992), 10.

chapter three

COMMUNICATING VISION BY GOING PUBLIC

By Bill Hybels with Valerie Bell

Casting a vision publicly is a daunting challenge because it forces leaders to put precise wording to their passions. It can also be nerve-wracking because every leader knows that the words he or she is bursting to say may well be received negatively. While opposition is hard enough to deal with in one-on-one situations, it is far more difficult when a group is involved and there is the very real possibility of causing division.

This is why some leaders choke and decide not to take that risk. They don't give the vision talk. They don't paint the passion-producing picture. They intentionally stay out of harm's way and acquiesce to the status quo—all to avoid possible pain. How tragic (and gutless, I might add). Everybody loses when a church's vision remains fuzzy. Everybody pays for the leader's lack of courage.

Let me suggest a way to bolster a leader's courage and also build consensus before taking a vision public. First, the leader brings together whoever makes up the senior leadership team of the church: key staff members, lay leaders, elders, deacons, and so on. Then he or she says to this group, "Our people deserve clarity on the vision God has given us. They need to know what we're about and where we're headed. So let's meet for the next eight Saturday mornings and figure out together, under the direction of the Holy Spirit, where God wants us to lead this church.

"We'll start by studying Acts 2 and asking God to give us the pictures, ideas, and words that capture his vision for this church. Then when we present it publicly we will be of one heart and one mind, and hopefully, the rest of the congregation will buy in. If some people don't resonate with the vision, we can talk to them one-on-one and give them time to process the potential changes. If after that they decide not to join us, we will trust that there are other churches where they will feel more at home. But let's come to leadership consensus so we can present the clearest, strongest vision possible."

I've seen hundreds of churches all over the world work through this process. Though it requires a major investment of time and energy, and things may get a bit bumpy along the way, the payoff is huge. Inevitably there comes that day when the whole leadership core is united and clear about its vision. At that time, the point leader can communicate the vision to the entire congregation with passion and power. And if God has truly guided the process, the vision will ignite the church. People will say, "Finally we are not just doing laps. We have a course, we have a target, and we are free to move together into a God-honoring future."

The "who" matters. By that I mean that choosing the appropriate person to give the talk is very important. Around Willow Creek we are totally committed both to team leadership and to team teaching. But when it comes to who will stand in front of the Willow Creek congregation on Vision Night and articulate what we're about and where we're headed, we don't draw straws. We believe that job is the responsibility of the recognized point leader, the person responsible for overseeing the team, congregation, or organization.

At Willow, that would be me. Many times I've suggested to the elders and management team that we let someone else handle that responsibility, but they don't even let me finish my spiel. "It's your job, Bill," they are quick to remind me. "You're the person who has embodied the vision from the beginning. You're the one whose passion we need to see and hear and experience again and again. The congregation needs to know that you are still committed to this dream and still willing to lay your time and energy on the line for it." The "who" matters. Churches must think this through and get it right.

The "when" also matters. In my experience, there are starting points, midway points, and ending points in a ministry season that almost demand a vision talk. In the United States, and particularly in the Midwest, our ministry season tends to run from September to Christmas. There's a brief Christmas break, when people are focused on family, travel, and holiday events, but then it typically fires up again from January to the end of June. The months of July and August, prime vacation months for Americans, force a natural lull in ministry momentum.

> Most leaders think that if they fill people with vision once, they'll stay full forever.

So, with these seasons in mind, I start the new ministry year with a vision talk in early September. Then in January, I do another vision talk. One January I did a vision talk called *The Soul of Willow Creek*. I delivered it at our weekend services because I wanted everyone, including seekers, to know who we are and where God is leading us. I wanted to give them a glimpse into the soul of Willow.

People loved it.

Two weeks later, at our midweek New Community services, we had our formal Vision Night where I recast the vision in greater detail. When I'm asked how often the vision should be publicly shared in an organization or in a church, I usually remind leaders that vision *leaks*. Most leaders think that if they fill people with vision once, they'll stay full forever. But that's just not true. Vision leaks, even out of our best people. The demands of everyday life gradually cause their minds to grow fuzzy, their commitment to wane, and their hearts to grow cold.

Effective leaders are always monitoring vision leakage. They stand ready to recast the vision whenever necessary. Most leaders, frankly, don't cast the vision enough. They blame followers for faltering commitment, not realizing that they have faltered in their role of vision caster.

PEOPLE NEED TO KNOW THE MAIN THING

One more piece of counsel about going public with the vision: Keep it simple. What I'm saying here might be a tad controversial, but I've thought a lot about this. These days so much is being written about the technical distinctions between vision, mission, and purpose that some leaders feel compelled to have separate statements for each. For years, we too attempted to make these distinctions. But in the end, I think it produced more confusion than clarity in our congregation. People would say, "What's our vision? Oh, I thought that was our purpose. No that was our mission. I give up!"

To avoid this kind of mess, leaders should remember this simple rule. *When a leader is casting vision publicly the goal is to help people to know, understand, and remember the "main thing."*

Call it vision, purpose, mission, or whatever. But people better be able to walk away saying, "I know the main thing." At Willow Creek the main thing has always been "to turn irreligious people into fully devoted followers of Christ." And I don't ever want anybody at Willow to get fuzzy on this.

Peter Drucker says the main thing should be able to fit on the front of a T-shirt. That means it better be crisp. It better be repeatable. It better be the kind of statement the average layperson can recite back with minimal trouble. If it's a paragraph long, it's probably not repeatable. It has to be succinct and memorable. That's why we have stuck with the nine words we came up with twenty-seven years ago: *Turning irreligious people into fully devoted followers of Christ.*

VISION INCREASES ENERGY AND MOVES PEOPLE INTO ACTION

Sounds like a lot of work, doesn't it—crafting a rally cry? Maybe you're reading this and wondering if, after all the effort, anything would really be different? It's a fair question. "What will improve if I get clear on our vision and communicate it compellingly to my people?"

Let me frame it this way. Most churches are full of wonderful, good-hearted people (better than some of us leaders, for sure). But life has a way of sucking the zest out of them. Careers, kids, responsibilities, and financial pressures combine to overload them physically and emotionally. Eventually life begins to feel to them like a backbreaking grind. The last thing they want to do is add serving at church to their to-do list. But an energizing, God-honoring vision can change all that. I've seen it happen many times at Willow. I saw it happen again just recently.

I met a twenty-something guy who told me how dull his life had become. He had been hanging around at Willow, but he hadn't gotten plugged in anywhere. Then he heard Sue Miller, our director of children's ministry, cast her vision about ministering to kids. He heard her speak of how noble it is to serve and love kids, to lead them to Christ, and then to grow them up in faith. She challenged people to give their lives to nurturing and developing children. The vision she cast about the value of kids ignited this young man into action. Now he's a committed volunteer in *Promiseland,* our children's ministry.

> "what will improve if I get clear on our vision and communicate it compellingly to my people?"

I bumped into him a month after our first meeting and he was lit up like a Christmas tree. He described the eight kids in his *Promiseland* small group. He knew their names, their families, their stories. Now his life is far from dull.

The same thing happened recently when I ran into a couple in the hallway outside my office. They said, "We were around Willow for years, attending but not doing much else. Then we heard a leader in the small groups ministry cast a vision about the value of community and about what it would mean to invest our lives in shepherding a small group of people."

They were so energized by that vision that they went through the training to become small group leaders. With great animation they said, "Our lives now revolve around leading our small group. It's the most important and exciting thing we do."

That's the power of vision. It creates energy that moves people into action. It puts the match to the fuel that most people carry around in their hearts and yearn to have ignited. But we leaders must keep striking that match by painting compelling kingdom pictures. Again, the leadership gift is the only gift that provides this energizing spark for the church. So we need to get this right.

VISION INCREASES OWNERSHIP

The second payoff of casting vision effectively is increased ownership. One of my fears related to vision is that someday our key leaders—board members, elders, management team, and lay leaders—will hear of an upcoming Vision Night and they'll yawn and say, "Been there, done that."

But the truth is, whenever I recast the vision to Willow, not only will new folks resonate, respond, and make our vision theirs, but inevitably, the faithful core upon whose shoulders Willow has been carried for so long will enthusiastically recommit. Veterans often make their way down to the bullpen where I stand after services and say, "Sign me up for another year. You can count on me. I'm more motivated by what we're doing together as a church than I ever have been before. I can't bear the thought of missing any part of the action." Seeing the clear picture again deepens their sense of ownership.

After a recent vision talk one of the founders of Willow, a man who's seen and heard it all, approached me and, with his finger to my chest, announced, "Bill, they're gonna have to take me out of here in a box." Translated: "I'm going to give the rest of my life to the vision of this church. I'm not going anywhere. I'm not going to lose heart. If the battle gets hard, I'm not going to quit. I'm here 'til the end. You can count on me." A commitment like that is one of the results of effective vision casting.

VISION PROVIDES FOCUS

A third benefit of vision casting is that it provides focus. A clear articulation of what a particular church is about also offers, by implication, a clear statement about what it *isn't* about. In other words, every vision that is cast embraces certain essential activities, but it also excludes scores of other energy-diverting activities. These excluded activities may be good in and of themselves, but if they are unrelated to the specific vision of a particular church, pursuing them will do more harm than good. Nothing neutralizes the redemptive potential of a church faster than trying to be all things to all people. It is impossible for any one church to do it all.

Leaders at Willow have been asked hundreds of times why we have never started a Christian day school. Our answer has remained the same from the beginning: we have never sensed God's prompting to head down that road. That being the case, we have been able to focus with greater intensity on evangelism and discipleship, both of which we have clearly sensed to be closer to the bull's-eye of God's vision for us.

A clear vision provides a compelling picture of the future that enables us to say, "We know our destination. Nothing will lure us off the path from here to there. We will not be distracted."

Leaders who realize the importance of actualizing their church's collective vision will unapologetically say "no" to all sorts of competing endeavors. Why? So that some day they can hear these words: "You stayed true to the vision I gave you. You didn't get sidetracked. You reached the unique destination I had in mind for your church. Well done! Well done!"

So the payoffs of a clearly defined vision are increased energy, increased ownership, and increased focus. Without being morbid, allow me to mention just one final payoff of painting a clear vision for the church: it reduces the trauma of leadership succession.

I won't be the senior pastor of Willow Creek forever. The human death rate still hovers around a hundred percent, and I doubt that I will be an exception to that statistic. Neither will you. So, we both need to understand that one of the greatest gifts we leaders can give our churches is a clear, God-honoring vision that will outlast us. Someday the elders of Willow Creek will begin the search for the next senior pastor. I fully expect that they will approach the candidates and say, "Here's what Willow is about. Here's the picture that produces passion at Willow. Here's the main thing that God has assigned us to do.

"We are a church with a white-hot commitment to turning irreligious people into fully devoted followers of Christ. We're united around that vision. We're energized by it. We own it. And we have laser-like focus. So if our vision and your vision are in sync and God leads you to become our next senior pastor, all you'll have to do is step into place, keep the rockets lit, and have a ball flying with us into the future."

Every four or five years, there's a ninety-degree vision change when a new pastor comes.

Wouldn't that be a wonderful way to pass a leadership baton? Wouldn't the bride of Christ be well served if we could sustain vision even during leadership transitions?

But what happens in most churches? Every four or five years, there's a ninety-degree vision change when a new pastor comes. Long-time church members know deep down that "this too shall pass." No wonder they eventually cross their arms and say, "We're not going to get on board with this vision. Before we even figure out what it means there will probably be a new one in place. Why should we bother to get serious about it?" I've seen entire congregations commit themselves to noninvolvement because of their frustration with revolving-door pastors and shifting visions. And I can't say I blame them.

But it doesn't have to be this way. Just as clear vision creates energy, increases ownership, and provides focus, it can also help churches maintain momentum and effectiveness during the critical process of passing the baton from one leadership team to the next.

A PAYOFF WRITTEN ON FACES

A few years ago I asked our video team to tape the part of our baptism service where new adult believers are immersed in the lake on our church property. With a song written by one of our vocalists used as background music, the video team created a three-minute video clip that is the most moving celebration of life transformation I have ever seen.

I decided to show the video at the annual Christmas party we have for our elders and board of directors. After enjoying a beautiful dinner I stood up and said, "Friends, I want to say thank you for serving for another year here. I want you to understand how very much I appreciate and love you. I thought the greatest gift I could give you tonight would be a visual image of the main thing that we're about. So just sit back and enjoy what you're going to see during the next few minutes."

Since I had already seen the video several times during the editing process, I was free to look into the faces of our senior leaders, those men and women who for so many years have carried heavy ministry loads with uncommon faithfulness. I wish you could have seen the energy, the joy, the determination, and the sense of fulfillment evident on their faces. I think their hearts were forming a silent choir singing, "Yes! This is our main thing. This is what God has called us to do. This is what we want to be about for the rest of our lives."

> It was the kind of moment leadership teams live for, the kind of moment only a crystal-clear vision can produce.

When the video clip ended, we looked into each other's tear-filled eyes and just sat there for several minutes in blissful silence, bathed afresh in God's vision for our church. It was the kind of moment leadership teams live for, the kind of moment only a crystal-clear vision can produce.

Vision. It's the most potent weapon in a leader's arsenal. It's the weapon that unleashes the power of the church.

Bill Hybels serves as senior pastor of Willow Creek Community Church in South Barrington, Illinois. Willow Creek's outreach to spiritual seekers in the Chicago area has made it one of the most attended churches in North America. Hybels has authored many books, including *Inside the Mind of Unchurched Harry and Mary* (Zondervan,1993), with Lee Strobel; and *Too Busy Not to Pray* (InterVarsity Press, 1998), with Lavonne Neff.

chapter four

SPEAKING INTO CRISIS

by gordon macdonald

I have long been romanced by the story of paul's bold intervention among the soldiers and sailors in charge of a ship that was breaking up in the middle of a mediterranean storm. Having exhausted their routine responses to severe conditions, they had given up hope of being saved.

Enter paul! "men," (and i'm paraphrasing here) "you should have listened to me earlier when i said not to leave port, but you didn't. But don't be afraid. I've received a word from god. The good news is that no life is to be lost; the bad news is that the ship has made its last voyage. Keep courageous, men; god will do as he's promised." Here was a voice speaking confidently into crisis, offering a message that steadies people and provides reliable direction. It's an apt subject for our times in which people are scared, wonder about the future, and speculate on their personal security. Not always the most important issues, ultimately, but nevertheless the ones on people's minds.

In times of crisis, people listen for a voice. They're tuned to receive messages of hope, courage, God's purposes, and meaning. Augustine's was such a voice when Rome was coming apart. Luther's was heard when the Holy Roman Empire was crumbling. Wesley's spoke into the turbulent times of the industrial revolution.

More recently two insightful voices spoke into the crisis in Germany during the 1930s and 1940s. Amid the economic, political, and military upheaval, only a few stood to speak for God. Among them: Dietrich Bonhoeffer and Helmut Thielicke. The two stand like human bookends at the beginning and the end of World War II. Bonhoeffer's greatest years were from 1932 to 1945, while Thielicke ascended to his prime in the mid-war years and those that followed.

It was given to Bonhoeffer to warn the German people of the political and moral consequences should they select Hitler as their national leader and then follow him to his grave. Thielicke's task was to challenge the German people to the task of spiritual and moral reconstruction. Both men did their jobs admirably.

THE COST OF DIETRICH'S DISCIPLESHIP

In 1933, just two days after Hitler became Chancellor of Germany, Bonhoeffer preached on the radio, warning of a leader "who allow(s) himself to succumb to the wishes of those he leads, who will always seek to turn him into their idol, then the image of the leader will gradually become the image of the 'misleader'…This is the leader who makes an idol of himself and his office, and who thus mocks God." Bonhoeffer was cut off the air as he spoke, presumably by Hitler sympathizers, and he was forced to publish the talk in print to make sure that his audience heard everything he had to say. But he'd made his stand, and soon there were those who questioned his patriotism.

His preaching and his instruction to student preachers took on an increasingly confrontive tone. "Do not try to make the Bible relevant," he said. "Its relevance is axiomatic…Do not defend God's Word, but testify to it…Trust to the Word. It is a ship loaded to the very limits of her capacity."

Bonhoeffer's greatest books come out of this era. *The Cost of Discipleship* called for one to pursue the selfless life, or, to use a more modern phrase, Bonhoeffer was trying to say, "It's not about me!

"The cross is laid on every Christian," Bonhoeffer wrote. "As we embark upon discipleship…we give over our lives to death."

In 1939 Dietrich Bonhoeffer visited New York, and friends in the church world passionately tried to keep him there for fear that if he returned to Germany, he would lose his life. But Bonhoeffer chose to sail back to Germany.

"I will have no right to participate in the reconstruction of Christian life in Germany after the war if I do not share the trials of this time with my people," he said.

"Christians in Germany will face the terrible alternative of either willing the defeat of their nation in order that Christian civilization may survive, or willing the victory of their nation and thereby destroying our civilization. I know which of these alternatives I must choose; but I cannot make that choice in security."

> DO not defend god's word, but testify to it...Trust to the word.

In the wartime years that followed, Bonhoeffer's logic led to relationships with people (including members of his extended family) who plotted to take Hitler's life. When they were almost successful, many were arrested throughout Germany, including Bonhoeffer, and he spent his last years in prison before being executed at Flossenburg in 1945, shortly before the war ended.

Even in prison, Bonhoeffer was ever the preacher. At one point he reflected on the hope generated in a fresh Christian marriage. "Welcome one another, therefore, as Christ welcomed you, for the glory of God," he quoted from the Scriptures, then expounded: "In a word, live together in the forgiveness of your sins, for without it no human fellowship, least of all a marriage, can survive. Don't insist on your rights, don't blame each other; don't judge or condemn each other, don't find fault with each other, but accept each other as you are, and forgive each other every day from the bottom of your hearts."

The larger significance of these comments is that Bonhoeffer never accepted the notion that life is only about the crisis. Rather, life goes on, and the more hopeful, new-start-oriented statements we can make—like marriage—the better.

Bonhoeffer was one tough preacher, and he called people to resistance against evil, to courage, to nobility of life and witness, to pure fellowship among Christ-following people.

"Who stands fast?" Bonhoeffer wrote in 1943. "Only the man whose final standard is not his reason, his principles, his conscience, his freedom, or his virtue, but who is ready to sacrifice all this when he is called to obedient and responsible action in faith and in exclusive allegiance to

God—the responsible man, who tries to make his whole life an answer to the question and call of God." Where are these responsible people?

Bonhoeffer was even preaching when they came to take him away to the place of execution. In his last hours, he was asked to speak to the prisoners. At first reluctant, Bonhoeffer relented. The text, from Isaiah, was "by his stripes we are healed."

Then he was led to the gallows, where after his execution, his biographer records, "His body was taken down and burned, along with his suitcase and manuscript." His manuscript! Bonhoeffer never stopped preaching and writing, even in the worst of times.

SERMONS IN A BOMBED-OUT CHURCH

If Bonhoeffer's calling was to warn the German people of the consequences of Hitler's political philosophy, Helmut Thielicke's calling was to sustain people through the war and then to help them rebuild their lives spiritually and morally afterward.

In 1936 Thielicke was awarded a professorship at the University of Heidelberg. But four years later, he lost his position when the Nazis became sensitive to his growing criticisms of the Hitler regime. He eventually moved to St. Mark's Church in Stuttgart, where he preached despite changes in venue from week to week due to damage from Allied bombing. John Doberstein, Thielicke's English translator, says that after each sermon hundreds of volunteer stenographers remained and took down dictated excerpts, which they then duplicated privately. Printing was forbidden, but these copies of the Christian message, handed from person to person, found their way to thousands of eager readers.

At one point during the war, Thielicke felt in desperate need of rest. He reasoned that some weeks spent in a quiet village in the countryside would be good medicine. Yet the retreat to the country failed to restore him, and he soon returned to the city. Yes, the village had been peaceful. But something was missing, which left him restless.

He concluded that people in the village were of a different mind, not deeply touched (yet!) by the war. And he craved to return to the city where people were clawing for survival. Among them he found a spiritual strength and vitality that was far more restorative than the "escapist" life of the countryside. So Thielicke returned to the bombs, the damage, and the suffering. Because there he found reality and courage and community. And that became the seedbed of much of his preaching.

"I have been interested in the theological question of what change takes place in a man," writes Thielicke, "when he finds God and so also finds himself. For of one thing I was always sure, that when a man seeks himself, he fails to find himself, and that he gains and realizes himself only when he loses his life in God."

He was bold when he called men and women to Christ. "I believe," he said, "that one can do justice to the seeker only if one leaves him under no illusions about the existence of a steep wall at which decisions must be made. He must be led to face the granite greatness of a message that brooks no evasion."

> what change takes place in a man when he finds god and so also finds himself?

In another place: "Anybody who looks downward and measures himself by the weaknesses of his fellow men immediately becomes proud…" And again: "When a man really turns to God with a burdened conscience, he doesn't think of other people at all. There he is utterly alone with God."

Are his comments out of date? Or do they call us back to something that may be lost in our time of sermons that smack more of self-help than deep-spirited and thoughtful gospel. When we look for the voices that have spoken out most eloquently and spiritually since September 11, will we hear any of the substance that these two "bookends" gave to the German people? Some time after the war Thielicke visited the United States and toured the United Nations building in New York. When he was shown the "chapel" in the UN building, he was appalled. It was a room decorated by spotlights and little else.

"The spotlights were ignorant of what they were illuminating, and the responsible men who were invited to come to this room were not shown to whom they should direct their thoughts. It was a temple of utterly weird desolation, an empty, ruined field of faith long since fled…only here, where the ultimate was at stake, only here was emptiness and desolation. Would it not have been more honest to strike this whole pseudo temple out of the budget and use the space for a cloakroom or a bar?"

The man was a prophet.

WHAT DO THEY SAY TODAY?

What can we say of these two World War II "bookends"? Certainly that they in fact did speak into their crisis. They were tough on their hearers; they expected much from the people to whom they preached and wrote. Their preaching was not parochial, pandering to the fears and superficial patriotism of their people. And they were willing to accept the consequences that came from proclaiming biblical truth.

For Bonhoeffer, this meant not just proclaiming but living out the message that ministry is more important than security. Instead of escaping the place of danger, he stayed where he could do the most good and paid the ultimate price for doing so.

Likewise, I hear Thielicke saying that the greatest preaching is most likely to come from the lips of a preacher who suffers alongside his or her people. We are not called—neither preacher nor hearer—to run fearfully from affliction or to curse it (and those who cause it), but rather to stand and face it, to squeeze from it everything God might like to say to us.

> *preachers may need to help some hearers understand that terrorism has been around for a long time in other parts of the world.*

In the wake of the horror of the World Trade Center/Pentagon attacks, we need to ask ourselves some challenging questions. Who speaks for God now? And how is his message heard, both in the churches and in the larger public? Billy Graham's eloquent remarks at the National Cathedral on September 14, 2001, will (or should) long remain a textbook in prophetic preaching. In a few brief moments the raspy and aging voice of this Christian statesmen called the country to alertness, courage, grace, and truth.

We need such voices that are tender, firm, thoughtful, timeless, and candid enough to call us to a life higher than the ordinary.

What we don't need are voices that speak out in vindictiveness, even, supposedly, in the name of biblical truth. It's not a time to blame various people groups with the word *evil* or *warlike* (a selective reading of our Older Testament will not make the Jewish/Christian tradition look too peaceable either). It isn't a time to take advantage of people's fears to raise money or prestige.

Speaking into crisis means focusing on themes such as

- *Hope* because people wonder if there is a tomorrow.

- *Courage* because people succumb too easily to fear.

- *Nobility* in the normal Christian life because living for the glory of God is our calling every day, but especially in times of crisis, and because loving (and forgiving) one's enemies is imperative.

- **Repentance** in those circumstance where we have come across as an arrogant and materialistic nation.

- **Biblical justice** because so few of us really understand what it is.

- And what **substantial prayer** looks and sounds like—praying for the leaders of this world, for peace, for those who suffer far more than we do.

Finally, how would a larger, God's-eye-view perspective on world events take shape in preaching? The horror of the World Trade Center losses (some three thousand people dead), as New York Mayor Rudolph Giuliani put it, is unbearable. But Christians need to be reminded by their preachers that as many as seven times that number (mostly children) die every day in the world because of disease and malnutrition. Additionally, preachers may need to help some hearers understand that terrorism has been around for a long time in other parts of the world. We simply cared too little when it was inflicted upon others not of our nationality.

But the most important theme to speak into crisis is theological at its base. It is to preach the sovereignty of a great and powerful God, of a Christ who weeps over the city (or the country, and not ours only) and who longs to come again to create a new heaven and a new earth. This kingdom-dream leaps off the pages of Scripture from beginning to end and tells us that life and relationship will be better, much better than we know today, when everyone shall bow to confess him as Lord of all.

What a day that shall be! And what a privilege to preach about it in the midst of crisis.

This chapter is adapted from an article originally appearing in Lead-ershipJournal, © 2002 by Gordon MacDonald. Used by permission.

Gordon MacDonald was senior pastor at Grace Chapel, Lexington, Massachusetts, for nineteen years. Now he is editor-at-large of Leadership and lives in New Hampshire. MacDonald is also the author of many books, including *Ordering Your Private World* (Thomas Nelson, 2003 revised edition).

chapter five

PREPARATION: THE KEY TO EFFECTIVE PREACHING

BY Thomas K. Tewell

ne of my predecessors at Memorial Drive Presbyterian church in Houston, which I served before coming to Fifth Avenue, was the Rev. Dr. Charlie Shedd. A master at communication, Charlie wrote many books on marriage and family life. Early in their marriage, he and his wife Martha taught a course titled simply "How to Raise Children." They taught that course before they had any children. After they had children, they taught the same class and titled it "Suggestions on Raising Children." Then when their children were teenagers they taught the same class but titled it "Feeble Hints from Fellow Strugglers"!

In this article, I want to share some feeble hints from a fellow struggler about the task of preaching. I believe there's no greater privilege in the ministry than preaching the gospel of Jesus Christ. It's overwhelming to think that God has entrusted to us the message of reconciliation (2 Corinthians 5:19)! Preaching demands our full concentration and attention—it must be one of the highest priorities of our ministry. If we make it a priority, we'll reap tremendous spiritual dividends for our congregations and for ourselves. The key to life-changing *preaching* is *preparation*. There's no substitute for preparation.

This may be the most important and yet most often overlooked aspect of preaching. Preparation means that I must be right in my relationship with God if I'm going to preach with passion and power. So I ask myself:

Am I in sync with God? How is my soul? How is my prayer life? Have I taken time to read devotionally as well as theologically as I prepared this sermon? Am I in sync with my wife, Suzanne; my two sons, Ryan and Toby; my daughter-in-law, Holly; my three grandchildren, Nathan, Hope, and Tyler; as well as the people on our staff and in our congregation?

Is my life in balance? Have I had a Sabbath day to recharge my batteries for ministry? Am I getting regular exercise? Am I getting enough rest? Do I take the time to do things that I enjoy other than ministry?

If I'm not right with God, myself, and the significant people of my life, I'm not ready to preach! As the Rev. Dr. Lloyd Ogilvie, chaplain of the U.S. Senate, has said so often, "Nothing happens through you until it happens to you." Thus, preachers cannot take their congregations further than they have gone in their own spiritual lives.

During my ministry studies, Dr. Neill Q. Hamilton, continuously referred to the writing of Peter Drucker in his lectures. Hamilton felt that Drucker shed a very helpful light on the dilemma facing the pastor and quoted Drucker as saying that the three most challenging professions today are the president of a college or university, the CEO of a hospital, and the pastor of a church.

> If I'm not right with god, myself, and the significant people of my life, I'm not ready to preach!

A pastor, a CEO of a hospital, and a university president must not only be good in one-on-one relationships and in small groups but must be able to command the attention of a large audience or congregation as well. In addition, they must be good at fund raising, management, delegation, supervision, and communication. They must see the big picture and be attentive to small details. They must get back to people promptly and be kind and sympathetic—while at the same time being strong and directive enough to command respect. In short, the demands are completely unrealistic!

But in the parish ministry, all pastors must do this every single week of their lives! Pastors must be ready to handle—with God's help—anything that hits them on any given day. Thus, the preparation of a pastor's personal life is also an important part of preparation.

I love the words of Bishop Quayle, who summarized this point more profoundly than I can when he said: "Is preaching the art of making a sermon and delivering it? Why no...Preaching is the art of making a preacher, and delivering that! Preaching is...the amassing of a great soul so as to have something worthwhile to give—the sermon is the preacher up to date." (Bishop Quayle, an American Methodist Bishop, quoted in Paul Sangster's biography of his father, W.F. Sangster)

PREPARING THE SERMON

People who don't make speeches every few days often don't understand the hours of reading, exegesis, and study as well as the writing and rewriting that go into effective sermons. I'm intentional about letting church leaders know that in my weekly schedule fifteen to twenty hours (minimum!) must go into the preparation of a sermon. I ask them to help me protect my priorities of study and preparation for my own good and for the good of the congregation.

The particular time of day when I study has been different in every congregation I've served. A preacher must find a rhythm of schedule that works. In my current church, I find that my time in the office is not effective for sermon preparation, so I try to do all my study for the day at home before I come to the church office. My goal is to study for one to three hours on most mornings. If I get up early, I can have a couple hours of uninterrupted sermon preparation before getting to the office at nine or ten. In addition, my goal is to take the better part of one day per week (usually Wednesday or Thursday) for actual sermon writing and rewriting.

Although all of this sounds great in theory, it doesn't always work perfectly in my busy life as a pastor. However, I find that if I have a rhythm to my life and a goal of when I want to prepare the sermon, it's easier after an emergency or a crisis to return to order rather than to return to chaos!

My goal is to finish my sermon and have it ready to preach on Thursday evening. I learned this from the Rev. Dr. John Galloway, who developed a Thursday-night worship service at Fox Chapel in Pennsylvania years ago. I once asked John, "How did you become such an effective preacher?" My friend replied that the Thursday evening service had dramatically improved his preaching. He would get his sermon ready and deliver it on Thursday night.

The attendance was small and after a few years the service was discontinued. However, Dr. Galloway realized that when he had the sermon ready to deliver Thursday night, he had Friday and Saturday to "stir the pot" and improve the message for the larger congregation on Sunday. Often, driving home from the church on a Thursday night, he would ask himself, "Why did I open with that illustration? What was I thinking when I ended the sermon that way? Why didn't I realize that the transitions just didn't work?" By Friday noon he had a greatly improved message! Then it was in his heart and soul throughout the weekend as he performed a wedding, watched a game, or went about his pastoral duties. By Sunday morning he could deliver the sermon without notes because he was so familiar with it. John's experience inspired me.

> preaching excellence is dependent on hours of study, thought, writing, rewriting, and prayer.

Although I rarely have the sermon completely ready to preach on a Thursday night (I once did it in 1995!), it has been extremely helpful to me to try to do so. If I have the sermon "almost ready" on Thursday night, then God's spirit can refine the sermon and me. Once I get the sermon completely ready, I go back over it and look for places for strengthening and improvement. Sermons get stronger with more rewriting, editing, and refinement. Week in and week out, preaching excellence is dependent on hours of study, thought, writing, rewriting, and prayer.

Preparing the illustrations

An illustration is the "icing on the cake" of an effective sermon...but it's not the cake itself! Preachers, myself included, often make the mistake of building an entire sermon around one illustration. Or they over-illustrate a message. When I use illustrations, I try to remember the folowing principles:

> • ***Do not use an illustration too quickly.*** When I find a great illustration, I'm tempted to use it the following Sunday. My experience has taught me to save it. Illustrations are like beef that needs to marinate over time. As good as that illustration may seem today, it may not relate all that well to the biblical passage that one is exegeting that Sunday. However, when you let an illustration sit for weeks or months, it can be brought out and used when needed. I file illustrations under the biblical passages they relate to and under the themes of the illustrations. I also

keep a general file of illustrations. The key is to not force the illustration into a sermon like a square peg in a round hole but rather to allow the illustration to flow out of the text. When I allow an illustration to simmer, stirring it over time, it fits better into the sermon.

• *Practice.* I've made the mistake of thinking that I know an illustration so well that I don't need to spend much time on it. This is a grave mistake! The key to a good illustration is timing, passion, eye contact, and placing it in the sermon where it fits best. Practicing an illustration can help you cut extraneous material from it. I like an illustration to be streamlined, succinct, and tight.

Communicators tell us that we're most fully awake after a good laugh. Skilled communicators often use humor to set up a difficult point that they will try to make later.

• *Keep your eyes open.* When I'm on an airplane, watching a ballgame, or relaxing, I often "rip and read." I sort through periodicals, magazines, newspapers, and journals, and rip out articles that I think have relevance. Like most busy pastors, I receive many more periodicals and data than I could ever use. However, having information filed for retrieval is an invaluable resource.

• *Ask the congregation for help.* I regularly ask business leaders, graduate students, and other well-read and well-educated people to watch for illustrations, statistics, and examples that might help me. Many people will clip an article out of The Wall Street Journal for me or send me an e-mail with statistics they've just received at an economic conference. I've received helpful material from all over the country. Of course, the problem is sorting through it and deciding what is usable and unusable. Years ago Dean Arthur Adams of Princeton Theological Seminary taught us an important principle: "To make a great sermon, you have to discard some very good material. The better quality material you discard in your sermon preparation, the better will be the sermon."

> communicators tell us that we're most fully awake after a good laugh.

• *Read widely.* I have always tried to read works from a variety of authors and have often received helpful material from people with whom I might not agree theologically. I seek out authors who nourish my soul, and try to read everything they write; C.S. Lewis, Dietrich Bonhoeffer, Henri Nouwen, and Barbara Taylor are excellent examples. I seek out preachers who nourish my soul such as Lloyd Ogilvie, Fred Craddock, Jim Forbes, William Willimon, Earl Palmer, and Barbara Lundblad. I read their sermons and books and listen to their CDs and tapes. Although I never try to imitate someone else, I'm nourished by others' preaching, and they push my own preaching to new levels when I see and hear how they exegete a tough text. I also find biblical scholars whose writing and insights are helpful in my exegesis. Raymond Brown's commentary on John's Gospel and Walter Brueggeman's Old Testament commentaries have been invaluable resources for me.

As a resident of New York City, I often walk down a city street and let the city speak to me.

• **Become a student of the culture.** As a resident of New York City, I often walk down a city street and let the city speak to me. I take a pad and pen and just listen to the sounds of the city. It's a good idea to "exegete" the city while we're exegeting a text. For example, I might try to imagine what Amos the prophet might say to New York City and to the United States. In the beginning of his oracle, when he said to the people of Israel, "For three sins of Judah, even for four, I will not turn back my wrath" (Amos 2:4a), I try to imagine what a prophet on Fifth Avenue might say to business leaders walking the streets today.

• **Remember how much people bring to the sermon.** A few years ago I was preaching on "taking the name of the Lord thy God in vain" as part of a series on the Ten Commandments. I made reference to the Atlanta Braves pitcher John Rocker, who had made extremely derogatory comments about people riding the Number 7 train to Shea Stadium, regarding their sexual orientation, racial and ethnic backgrounds, and so on. When I got to that illustration, I began, "There's a pitcher for the Atlanta Braves..." Immediately people started to sigh, and I realized they didn't need an explanation of Rocker's comments. So I simply said, "You already know who I'm talking about!" and the congregation exploded in laughter. Then I said, "When we make

GREAT PREACHING

derogatory comments about any of God's children…we take the name of the Lord in vain." There was a noticeable "umm" from the congregation. I didn't need to say anymore. The congregation brought all they needed to that illustration.

Delivering the sermon without notes

Although I write out my sermons word for word, I never take that written manuscript into the pulpit. I always translate it into notes that will bring the key phrases to my mind. I rarely look at the notes in the pulpit and occasionally preach without them. At Memorial Drive Presbyterian Church in Houston, I preached at the early service with our youth choir of sixty to eighty high schoolers sitting around me. There was no place for a pulpit, lectern, or notes! Although it often felt as if I was walking a tightrope, the experience of preaching without notes made me a more effective preacher.

The key to preaching without notes is internalizing the message. Once I've fully internalized the message and made it my own, I'm free. Reciting a passage of Scripture or delivering a poignant illustration is far more powerful while looking people in the eye than looking at a manuscript. Eye contact can turn a good sermon into a great one.

Developing a weekly, monthly, quarterly, and annual rhythm

In the summertime, I block out several weeks to outline and prepare my sermons for the coming year. I think through the events of the year in our congregation and in our city. Will there be a major election? Are we on the brink of war? Are there major changes in the economy? What are the issues confronting our society, nation, city, and state? I wrestle with these questions in light of the lectionary texts for the coming year. Together they form the grist for the mill of my sermon preparation.

My goal is to think through the sermons I'm going to preach for an entire year (September through June). I try to have a Scripture, theme, possible title, and brief summary of where I'm going with each sermon by the end of August. I then distribute this information to Sunday school teachers, musicians, other pastors, and church leaders to help them with planning for the year ahead.

To prepare the congregation for messages to come, I put an outline of sermon titles and biblical texts in the bulletin for the upcoming month or two. Although not everyone reads it, those who do, find it to be a wonderful resource.

I try to cultivate a sense of anticipation and expectation so that people come to services expecting to hear God's voice. One way I do this is through creative sermon titles. I like titles that are provocative and appealing, particularly to "nonreligious types." I may choose a title that would appeal to a businessperson, such as "If the Apostle Paul Worked for Goldman Sachs" or "The Achilles' Heel of Corporate America." During Advent I may choose a title such as "The Empty Chair at Christmas Dinner" or "The Pain of Christmas," which taps into the loneliness that many feel at Christmastime.

These creative titles draw people in, but remember that the title comes *last*. It grows out of the development of the sermon. Believe me, I've made the mistake of hearing a great title and then trying to find a text for it! It might work for one sermon, but it doesn't work for the long haul. My best titles grow out of my study of the text. And I try to keep titles provocative and creative without being inappropriate or trite.

The goal of a good title is to get people thinking about the upcoming sermon so that they'll not want to miss it. I put my sermon titles on the signboard on Fifth Avenue, often creating a conversation piece for people passing by. When I was not in a congregation on such a busy thoroughfare, the upcoming sermon titles in the bulletin would have people in the congregation smiling, giggling, and wondering what each sermon was going to be about. I even know people who rearranged travel plans because of a carefully crafted title.

Part of the reason I work so hard at sermon titles is that I believe it's a sin to bore people in church! I believe the church of Jesus Christ should be the most exciting and dynamic place anyone could ever be.

Relating the biblical text to the daily concerns of people is another important aspect of preparing the congregation. Although it's extremely important to exegete the biblical text properly and share the historical and cultural background of a passage of Scripture, there's also no substitute for helping people relate the Scripture passage to their everyday lives. All of us as preachers need more creativity!

> The goal of a good title is to get people thinking about the upcoming sermon so that they'll not want to miss it.

I begin my study by opening the text and taking time to imagine what was going on in the text. I try to smell it, taste it, feel it, and imagine myself in the text. This technique, which I learned from Dr. Barbara Brown Taylor, has proved to be an invaluable resource in my preparation. In addition, I ask myself, "How will members of the congregation apply this text to their own lives?" If it's a text about money or material possessions, I try to remind myself that I'm in a congregation filled with investment bankers and people who trade stocks and commodities each day. I ask myself how they will "hear" this text. I also ask myself how it will be received by those who have just lost a loved one or those who are out of work, in transition, or dealing with depression or despair.

THE PRIVILEGE OF PREACHING

Years ago a family who had just heard the singing of Beverly Sills, the great Metropolitan Opera star, asked for her autograph back in her dressing room. She was only too happy to oblige. The father didn't know what to say after Ms. Sills had given the autograph. In his anxiety, he found himself saying, "We must go and let Ms. Sills rest. She has to sing tonight." Beverly Sills looked the father in the eye and said, "Oh no...I don't have to sing tonight." The father said, "Oh yes...look here in the program. '8 p.m., Beverly Sills, Featured Soloist'...it's right here in print." Beverly Sills said, "I don't *have* to sing tonight, I *get* to sing tonight! Do you know what a privilege it is to sing at the Metropolitan Opera? Do you know what a privilege it is to have the voice I've been given? It is an inestimable privilege, and I do not take it for granted. I savor every moment that I get to do this."

I feel the same way about preaching. We don't *have* to preach; we *get* to preach! Doesn't such a privilege demand our most serious preparation?

Thomas K. Tewell is senior pastor of Fifth Avenue Presbyterian Church in New York City and a trustee of Princeton Theological Seminary. Dr. Tewell has served pastorates in Bethlehem, Pennsylvania, and New Providence, New Jersey. He left the five-thousand-member Memorial Drive Presbyterian Church in Houston to become senior pastor at Fifth Avenue in September 1994.

chapter six

THE DYNAMICS OF SERMON DELIVERY

BY E.K. Bailey and Warren W. Wiersbe

Suppose you attended a worship service in an African-American church in Birmingham or Boston, in Chattanooga or Chicago, then the following Sunday you attended a service in a predominantly Caucasian congregation, and you were asked to describe the styles of sermon delivery. Or suppose you were visiting in a city away from your home. So you turned on the television in the hotel room where you were staying and caught a half hour of a white service followed by a black service. What differences might you see? How might the styles of sermon delivery differ? It has been said, "Black preaching is a dialogue that does not occur after but during the sermon. It is a call-and-response style of communication coming out of the African tradition. The congregation is encouraged and expected to participate in the act and art of preaching with verbal and body response."[1] Is that an accurate characterization, or a stereotypical generalization?

Sitting in the lounge of the Concord Missionary Baptist Church in Dallas, we asked E.K. Bailey and Warren Wiersbe:

■ *What's unique about sermon delivery in the black community as compared to the white community?*

Bailey: I think there are similarities and differences. I think that all effective preaching tries to internalize the text to the point that when it is preached, the listener experiences the text. In his book *Celebration and Experience in Preaching,* Dr. Henry Mitchell says that the preacher's task is to provide a total experience of the gospel. The experience-centered gospel stimulates the growth of gut-level trust in God by providing involvement and encounters where faith had and has been caught and taught. Black preachers want to get into the text and feel it, touch it, taste it, smell it, rub shoulders with it, and then allow the people to experience the trust of the text.

Wiersbe: I think anything unique anywhere depends on the preacher and the church. The black community may be a different context altogether, because the congregation is an important part of the preaching. But too often we preachers in the white churches preach the way they expect us to preach. If I go to Third Reformed Church to speak, I probably wouldn't preach the way I would at Concord Church. Is there a consistent delivery from church to church in the black community? I didn't think so.

Bailey: No, it depends on the church and the pastor. People gravitate to the church and the preacher that best fit their values, expectations, or comfort zones.

■ *Is there anything unique about the approach to sermon delivery?*

Bailey: I think that in the African-American churches, the preacher has much more freedom. We are freer in what we can do and what we can say and how long we can take to say it.

Wiersbe: Charismatics have moved in that direction.

Bailey: Yes, they have.

Wiersbe: The charismatics have defrosted a lot of churches. We may not totally agree with their theology, but they have helped to bring new life to many churches.

Bailey: Especially in sermon delivery. They've helped to reignite the emotive aspect, which has been positive because it allows the whole person to worship and the whole person to preach. So I think that has enhanced preaching, because the participatory relationship between pulpit and pew enforces the creative moment. It results in adding creativity and spice to help get the people involved in the preaching experience. The freedom that the black preachers have always enjoyed I see spilling over into some of the white churches, especially, as you said, the charismatic churches.

THE PLACE OF EMOTION AND EMOTIONALISM

■ *Let's expand on that idea. What's the place of emotion in preaching, both positive and negative?*

Wiersbe: Well, the negative of emotion is emotionalism, and we don't want that. We don't want ham actors in the pulpit. Emotionalism is artificial. It's made for the moment.

Bailey: Manipulative.

Wiersbe: It's when you stop communicating and start manipulating. That's so easy to do, even with an enthusiastic congregation. They'll go anyplace you lead them. The preacher needs the self-control that the Holy Spirit can give. There's always room for true emotion in worship and in preaching. To shed tears in the pulpit is not wicked, but in some churches, the people would be embarrassed.

Bailey: My people aren't ashamed of showing their emotions.

Wiersbe: My Swedish forebears were not afraid to cry publicly, but my German relatives were on the other end of the spectrum.

Bailey: Whether for good or ill, this is one of the lines of demarcation that has separated blacks and whites, because African-Americans historically have been and still are an emotional people. With us, celebration is a cultural thing, whether in church or at the football stadium. You can follow this all the way back to Africa. It wasn't until I visited Africa that I really began to understand why we are the way we are. For instance, wearing loud colors is an African tradition that we brought over with us. I don't necessarily agree with all these traditions, but you have to understand where they came from and what they mean. Even down to the bragging we do—"I'm the greatest!"

When Ricky Henderson won the base-stealing championship—he stole more bases than Lou Brock—and he lifted second base over his head, he was criticized for getting so emotional about it. There is a difference in the way blacks and whites celebrate. White folks need to know that my people are emotional, not to show off or get attention but because that's the way we are. If what Phillips Brooks said in his Yale lecture is true, that preaching is truth proclaimed through personality, then we must make room for the pathos of the preacher just as much as we make room for the logos and ethos.

SOLICITING
CONGREGA-
TIONAL
FEEDBACK

■ *How do you obtain and encourage congregational feedback and responsiveness to the sermons?*

Wiersbe: You read your mail, answer your phone, and don't stay at arm's length.

■ *There's responsiveness both during the sermon and afterward. How do you encourage that kind of back and forth?*

Wiersbe: I think that one of the keys is just plain openness to people. They realize you're not going to cut their throat if they say something negative. A.W. Tozer taught me a great lesson about criticism. He said, "Never be afraid of honest criticism. If the critic is right, he's helped you. If the critic is wrong, you can help him." Either way, somebody is helped. My best and most helpful feedback came from the staff and from the elders. They didn't feel that they had to pat me on the back or put me on a pedestal. They would talk quite frankly but lovingly. That was a big help to me. Our family can be a great help in this area.

Bailey: Sure. So far as the response to the preaching event, I think black preachers do have a unique experience, because we have the privilege to have a conversation within a conversation, while not losing sight of the first conversation as the second conversation is going on. Does that thoroughly confuse you?

Wiersbe: Well, the one conversation—pew to pulpit—enhances the other.

Bailey: One does enhance the other. While I'm preaching, I may stop and ask, "Have I got a witness? Are you still there? Do you hear what I'm saying?" But when I ask, "Do I have a witness?" I'm not really asking for a witness. I use it as a pacer. If I'm going too fast, it helps to slow me down. Or I use it as a pacer to give people time to intellectually breathe. Or I use it as a pacer to really ask for your support or to find out if you're paying attention. Black preachers have these two conversations going on at the same time. The conversation also builds a camaraderie that is just incredible between the pulpit and the pew. Now a lot of this has been dropped in some churches as our people have been exposed to the media and have heard other preachers, but by and large it still goes on. I still do it. But people are becoming more sensitive to the clock, so some of this two-way conversation may have to stop because of the time factor.

I don't get the kinds of letters that white pastors get. I've talked to some white pastors who tell me about the incredible letters they receive. When I initially began to receive a few letters, I was offended, because this was not a part of our history. I had some people from New York join our church. One lady had a Pentecostal background and wrote me, either with a compliment or a criticism, almost every Sunday. But some of her criticisms were on target, and I had to work my way through them because I wasn't accustomed to that sort of feedback. I finally called her in to sit down and talk about it, and she told me what her tradition was and I told her what mine was. She slowed her writing down to about once a month, but she kept it up. Once we had talked about it, I looked upon it much more favorably and accepted what she had to say. We eventually clashed over some doctrinal matters, and they left the church.

I don't think people have a right to criticize and remain anonymous; therefore, if a letter is signed, I'll read it and respond. If it is unsigned, my secretary reads it, and the letter usually ends up in the wastebasket. I've asked my secretary not to show me any anonymous mail.

> "If it's not worth signing, it's not worth reading."

Wiersbe: Dr. Harry Ironside, who pastored Moody Memorial Church in Chicago, used to say, "If it's not worth signing, it's not worth reading."

Bailey: Occasionally somebody will write and ask a real interesting question about the message, although we don't usually get a lot of feedback through the mail. What I've tried to do in the past to correct that was to pool together a preaching team that gives me evaluations and suggestions. Two of the members are my researchers; one of them is a member of my office staff, a lady, because I think it's important to get the female perspective.

Wiersbe: My wife sees things in the Bible that I don't see—and they're really there!

Bailey: A man and a woman can read the same text and never approach it the same way. So I'll ask her what she hears the text saying. And her input makes a lot of difference because most of our congregations have more women than men anyway. We constantly preach from the male side of the mental perspective, and it's important to hear what the women have to say.

■ *As a congregation becomes more affluent, does that alter the back-and-forth conversation? Do parishioners become more sedate, more controlled?*

Bailey: It can go either way. I know some African-American congregations that have become more sedate as they've become more affluent and better educated. It depends on how dear they hold their cultural background. The Concord Church is affluent and educated and adapts to all types of preaching, because the Word of God is central, yet we have not moved away from call and response. Despite the excess of some, and despite the massive rational, intellectual attack of the scholarly establishment, folk language has a way of clinging to the subtle wisdom and power that has been collected and funneled from generation to generation. So long as the generation's descendants speak the words, some portion of that original impact will insist on surviving. Per Dr. Henry Mitchell, the preacher who would tap this resource for redemptive contemporary ends needs only to join the life stream of the common folk and interpret the gospel from that population base's heritage, culture, and perspective. On the other hand, case in point, I know a black pastor friend who is as different from myself as night is from day, but our churches function in similar ways. The church I serve has more of an African-American culture, and where he serves has more of the flavor of the Eurocentric culture, but our churches offer a very similar approach to ministry. Both are committed to preaching the Word, but it's the "flavor" of the worship services and the philosophy of how to "do church" that makes us lean in two different cultural directions. People will make their decision based on what they're comfortable with.

HANDOUTS
AND
TESTIMONIES

■ *What about sermon handouts?*

Wiersbe: Make them available the next week. If you put the outline in the bulletin, the sermon becomes predictable, the surprise element is lost, and you can't make any last-minute changes.

Bailey: When I give an outline, it's the kind where you fill in the blanks.

■ *What about the use of testimonies in the service?*

Bailey: We do it.

■ *Does that help or enhance the preaching? What are some ways that you use testimonies?*

Bailey: Whenever I'm doing stewardship preaching, I use testimonies that tie into the sermon. I mean, it's incredible what God leads some people to say and do. One young lady, in her early thirties, was telling us that she wanted to give, but when she looked at her budget with her financial planner it just was not there. She downsized. She moved to a smaller apartment and bought a smaller car so she could give to the Lord.

Wiersbe: Amen.

Bailey: And that just floored us in light of where this generation is, to make that kind of sacrifice to give. Well, one of my members told me I needed to hear this young lady's testimony. I called her and she told me her testimony. I said, "You're on next Sunday." The impact was absolutely incredible. I've also used testimonies in the middle of the sermon. You have to work with the people and tell them they have only two minutes. If you don't cut it off, we'll cut you off! I tell them to write out the testimony and don't add anything to it. I've had only one person go a little bit over, but most of the time they stick with it once I work with them.

Wiersbe: The power of personal testimony is a marvelous thing. A ninety-year-old member of our church gave witness to our college department—between five and six hundred students—about how the Lord taught him and his wife to give. He had five minutes to tell the story. He came hobbling out, sat down on a stool, and talked for five minutes. Do you know what the students did when he was through? They gave him a standing ovation! You'd have thought they were at a football game. When the witness is authentic, people will show respect.

SHORTENED ATTENTION SPANS

■ *One of the shifts that affects preaching today is the short attention spans of the younger generations, especially those who watch MTV and who have hyperactive schedules. Should we shorten the length of sermons today? Is there a difference between the black and the white cultures when it comes to the length of services?*

Wiersbe: Well, they need more time than we do.

Bailey: Again, we're talking about change, and I'm struggling with this very thing. But my struggle is leading me toward shortening the sermons, which is making my sermons tighter and more effective. This is also in line with the changing times, because the hour of yesterday is the thirty seconds of today.

Wiersbe: Nothing wrong with that.

Bailey: Well, no, there's not. These changes in society, and the expectations of the younger congregation that I'm preaching to, can work out positively for my own ministry. I'm struggling with that because I was born into a culture where our preachers have been free to do it their way, and maybe their way needed some adjusting. I think it is important that we take into consideration the times that we're preaching in and the people that we're preaching to, as well as the various generational needs we should address. I don't think that these factors should dictate everything we do, but I choose to address these factors because it's making my preaching more effective. That's the whole purpose of preaching.

> I used to tell my students not to be "airplane preachers" who circle and circle but never land.

Wiersbe: I wish every preacher could be on the radio for a year and learn how to say it right the first time. I used to tell my students not to be "airplane preachers" who circle and circle but never land. If we work at it, we can say it right the first time. I think the entire service needs to be more disciplined. At the church we attend, we added fifteen minutes to each of the three Sunday morning services, which meant people had to be there at eight o'clock for the first service. That extra fifteen-minute margin has made a wonderful difference, and nobody has complained about having to get there fifteen minutes earlier. The same people who have been late for thirty years are still late. Without dumbing down the liturgy or moving at the speed of light, we can tighten up the total service and allow more time for preaching. Another important thing is that we hit that pulpit running and not waste time on long introductions.

EMBARRASSING MOMENTS

■ *What's the most embarrassing thing that has happened to you when you were preaching?*

Wiersbe: One of the embarrassing things that happened to me was caused by my own stupidity. I asked the congregation to turn to a reference that had no relationship whatsoever to the message. I had written down the wrong Scripture.

Bailey: The wrong Scripture. I've done that.

Wiersbe: My preaching professor, Dr. Charles Koller, used to tell us to get to church early each Sunday, make sure the participants in the service all have bulletins and know what's planned, and then check your references. Well, I didn't do that. I just said, "I'm sorry, folks, but this has nothing to do with my message." And we moved on.

Bailey: It's important to know how to recover from those kinds of mistakes and learn to laugh at yourself. If you're too serious about it, sometimes it will cause the whole sermon to bomb. When you laugh at yourself and call the people's attention to it, they'll laugh with you and not at you. In all my years of preaching without a manuscript, I have never had a memory lapse, but it happened to me one Sunday morning. I was preaching at the second service, and I could not recall the second point of my sermon. Fortunately, earlier in the week I had been watching Norman Vincent Peale on national television, and the same thing happened to him. He turned around and asked his assistant, "What is my second point?" And his assistant told him. In a similar fashion, when I forgot my second point, I turned around to my assistant, who always takes my notes, and asked him what my second point was. My assistant immediately responded with the appropriate answer. I turned back to the congregation and said, "Ladies and gentlemen, my second point is…!" They fell out of their seats laughing, and we moved right on.

Wiersbe: But there's one little factor you've left out: you have stature as a preacher, and so does Dr. Peale. That helps. In fact, people may enjoy seeing an expert make a mistake!

PREACHING FOR A VERDICT

■ *What about the idea of "preaching for a verdict"? Is that still valid today?*

Wiersbe: Many churches no longer give invitations for the lost to come and trust Christ.

Bailey: Well, I still do it, and I think it is still very important.

Wiersbe: I agree with you.

Bailey: Some younger seminary graduates have been taught that the public invitation is no longer appropriate. People are told to fill out a card, or come back Monday night for personal help, or they're encouraged to write the pastor or see someone after the benediction. I have never felt comfortable moving away from a public appeal. I think it's biblical.

Wiersbe: That isn't to say that there aren't other approaches or that they don't work. But why deliver your soul for thirty minutes or more and then not give people an opportunity for a personal response?

Bailey: Remember the old adage: "When the hunter raises the gun, look for some game to fall." If God is moving in hearts because of the message, he can call them right then and there. Let's give folks an opportunity to respond to the call of Christ.

> In preaching we inform the mind and stir the heart, but we also need to bend the will.

Wiersbe: The metaphor behind "preaching for a verdict" bothers me a bit. It's the picture of a lawyer confronting a jury that has the right to decide whether what we said was right or wrong. That's not the atmosphere that I want for preaching. Nobody has the right to vote on God's truth. To me, the metaphor of the invitation should be, "Come to the feast, come to the wedding! Don't stay where you are! Come to the feast!"

Bailey: In preaching we inform the mind and stir the heart, but we also need to bend the will. People don't change until the will has been bent. They must be willing to submit to God's Word and God's call. People do what they're moved and motivated to do, and that involves the mind, heart, and will. That's the key to the invitation.

Wiersbe: At Moody Church, we ended the service with a hymn, and it wasn't always one of the standard invitation hymns. I would invite anybody to come who sensed that God was calling. We had counselors ready to help them. After the service we held a visitors' reception, and we occasionally saw people come to Christ there. The elders would introduce visitors to me, and this gave me the opportunity to ask about their spiritual life. If at Pentecost, Peter had not called people to repent and believe but had offered to see them later that afternoon near the temple, I wonder if three thousand would have responded?

Bailey: At the same time, we should diversify the invitation, because there are people who can be reached through multiple approaches. Jesus told Peter to cast his net on the other side of the boat. If you fish with one pole, you're just going to catch one fish; however, if you use a net, you will have a better chance catching many fish at one time. Sometimes you need a net! Therefore, we use more than one approach to the invitation. We have people walking the aisles, we have response cards in the pews, and we also have what is called "Face to Face" at Concord, which is our reception for our guests.

Wiersbe: It also helps during the public invitation to have counselors up front to welcome those who come and to open the Word to them. Some of them should wait at the front after the service ends, just in case somebody is seeking help. Not all babies are born in public.

Bailey: If seekers prefer to fill out a card and leave it in the back of the pew, we follow up on that right away. At the guest reception the people have doughnuts and coffee, and not only do we tell them a little bit about who we are, but we also seek to explain who Christ is and the relationship he desires to have with them. Before they leave we offer another opportunity to accept Christ or make whatever commitment they need to make. Some people are comfortable doing this in a smaller gathering. The younger people are very comfortable with filling out cards and leaving them in the back of the pew, but it is different in each generation.

Wiersbe: Regardless of how we call people to trust Christ, we need to remember that the harvest is the end of the age, not the end of the meeting. We'll meet people in heaven who came to Christ because of some ministry of ours, and we knew nothing about it. God's Word accomplishes God's work in God's time.

<table>
<tr><td>CHANGES
THROUGH
THE YEARS</td><td>■ *All of this seems to be a part of this matter of change. What are some of the big changes you've seen during your years of ministry?*</td></tr>
</table>

Wiersbe: The ideal preacher fifty years ago expounded the Scriptures and gave you outlines and explanations. Today the emphasis in preaching is on meeting personal needs. When I was in seminary, the pastoral counseling movement was just taking hold. We read one book on the subject. But the impact of the pastoral counseling movement forced us to change our preaching and consider intent as well as content. I think that's the biggest change I've seen.

I think the second change is that local church ministry is no longer from the top down and only in the hands of the "experts," the trained preachers. A very healthy lay movement has developed and has greatly strengthened the church.

Bailey: The dominant changes in the African-American culture have been related to the struggle of having access to social and economic freedom. This struggle has been going on a long time, and as it has changed, our preaching has changed. We're not helping our people interpret the times in which we find ourselves, push back the horizons, and find out what the next steps should be. More African-American preachers have taken advantage of college and seminary training, and this has brought changes in the way we say things as we preach. Blacks have always preached salvation but didn't always use the same vocabulary as white evangelicals. I've met whites who didn't believe that blacks were saved, simply because we didn't use the traditional evangelical language. That's a horrible assumption to make. Even though we didn't express things the same way as the whites did, there was no question about the encounter our people have had with Jesus Christ. After going to school many of our preachers, including myself, have begun to use the best of the evangelical language. Some of the perceptions that were different in each of our cultures are now coming together because we're using the same language. The experience of salvation has always been there, but now we are starting to use the same language that communicates the salvific experience.

> I've met whites who didn't believe that blacks were saved, simply because we didn't use the traditional evangelical language.

Wiersbe: It seems to me that the black church over these years has been countercultural in its opposition to the white establishment, whereas the white church has not been the light it should have been. Our white churches have been mirrors reflecting the values of the culture instead of lights exposing the sins of the culture.

INTRODUCING
CHANGES IN
PREACHING

■ *How do you introduce changes in preaching without losing your congregation? Are there ways to prepare your leaders and your members for changes in preaching?*

Wiersbe: I've found that the best way to do something different in the pulpit is to introduce the change in another meeting. But don't keep doing this. Back off and then do it again. This enables you to test the waters. But if you're talking about major changes, then you'll have to sit down with your leaders and explain both the theology and the philosophy of the changes. If there's a book available that deals with these changes, have the leaders read it and then discuss it on a retreat. We must take a nonaggressive, nonmilitant posture so they don't think we're declaring war on some cherished tradition.

Bailey: I think that method is very good for making changes within the church's structure and program. However, in the African-American church the pulpit is the driving force for change. If seeds are not planted in the Word of God from the pulpit, they will seldom take root in the heart of the congregation.

Wiersbe: I'd have to say to my leaders, "Brethren, from time to time you're going to hear me approaching some texts from what you would call a social-action angle. We all believe it's biblical to preach about the sins of society. I'm not preaching some social gospel, but I am trying to apply the gospel to social needs." I'd want to be wise as a serpent but harmless as a dove.

Bailey: I do think that we should do some grunt work in this book for those pastors who have a heart but don't have a clue. How do I develop the same core values in my leadership? I tease the young preachers at our church with a quote: "First Bailey chapter one, verse one, 'There is a way that seemeth right to the young pastor, but the end thereof is to get put out.'"

Wiersbe: There's a difference between cosmetic changes—a new bulletin cover—and structural changes such as a whole new liturgy or a new organizational plan. Wise is that pastor who knows the difference and is unwilling to sacrifice his ministry just to achieve a small victory. We must have the right perspective and the right timing, or we'll create more problems than we'll solve. Also, when you make changes, you have to study the ripple effect. Who are the people affected? How will they respond? Will the changes be misunderstood?

■ *Picture a church that's been very traditional. The minister always sat on a platform, they followed the same order of service week after week, and he preached the same way every Sunday. Now this young pastor comes to the church and wants to introduce a testimony in the middle of his sermon. Or maybe he wants to back up the sermon with drama or do some first-person narrative preaching. What's your counsel?*

Wiersbe: Whether he's young or old, the new pastor should take time to get to know the people of the church, and especially the leadership, and to find out how changes are made in the church. Who are the people with the authority—and they aren't always the officers! If changes are forced from the outside, people will react negatively; but if they grow from the inside, they have a better chance of being accepted. The pastor who makes all those changes at once is in for trouble.

Bailey: I agree. The only thing that will change will be his address.

Wiersbe: Change for the sake of change is nothing but novelty. Change for the sake of better ministry and great outreach is progress. You can build a crowd with novelty, but you can't build a church.

Bailey: In the African-American church the preacher has greater influence and authority, and the leadership generally supports that kind of pulpit freedom if the pastor decided to change his approach. One exception might be if he moved the pulpit. That might create a problem, but even that is not the cardinal sin. But if preaching changes started to bleed over from the pulpit into the various programs and auxiliaries of the church—where things are very traditional and institutionalized—and the pastor tries to make sweeping changes there, then he would run into conflict.

> You can build a crowd with novelty, but you can't build a church.

Wiersbe: Church groups and officers can be very territorial. It's human nature. I heard about a Sunday school class that sued the church for asking them to move out of their room to another room. The class had bought and laid the carpeting, they had decorated the room and purchased furniture, and they had no plans to relocate.

Bailey: I know a church that had a battle with the Sunday school because the people were paying their tithes to their Sunday school classes and not to the church during the regular offertory period. Each adult class had a bank account separate from that of the church. The church mortgage was about to be foreclosed, and the Sunday school told the church, "That's your problem."

Wiersbe: Organizational problems are basically spiritual problems. Like some family problems, they're solved as the children grow up and get a mature outlook on things. The pastor needs to be patient and prayerful. We don't like to say it, but sometimes a funeral or somebody leaving the church helps to solve a problem.

NOTES

1. William Bailey McClain, "African-American Preaching," quoted in *Leadership Handbooks of Practical Theology,* vol. 1, *Word and Worship,* ed. James D. Berkley (Grand Rapids, MI: Baker, 1992), 76.

This chapter is from the book *Preaching in Black and White,* © E.K. Bailey and Warren W. Wiersbe (Zondervan, 2003). Used by permission.

E.K. Bailey is founder and senior pastor of Concord Missionary Baptist Church in Dallas. He has widely lectured and preached at conventions, seminars, churches, and seminaries around the world. His E.K. Bailey Ministries sponsors the annual National Conference on Expository Preaching. Warren W. Wiersbe, former minister of Moody Church and general director of *Back to the Bible,* is author of over 150 books, selling over four million copies. He travels widely as a conference preacher and speaker. He lives in Lincoln, Nebraska.

chapter seven

PREACHING FOR TRANSFORMATION, PART 1

BY crawford w. loritts jr.

I was born on february 11, 1950. That means, among many other things, that most of my formative years were spent on the front row of some of the most dramatic social changes of the last century.

I grew up in the context of "cause." I witnessed the struggles and triumphs of the civil Rights movement, culminating in the dismantling of legalized segregation. I heard some of the most powerful, eloquent speeches denouncing injustice and offering direction, solutions, and vision for the future. I also heard moving addresses calling for the radical overthrow of the "system" and status quo in our country. I saw and lived through tragedy. I was sitting in my junior high language class when we were told that president john f. kennedy had been shot. Then came the assassinations of president kennedy's brother bobby kennedy and martin luther king jr. In the evenings I sat in front of our television, struggling with feelings of anger, loss, and sadness as I saw cities being burned and gutted by race riots.

On the heels of the riots came the escalation of the war in Vietnam. Thousands of young men—a few whom I knew personally—lost their lives in a war that our country was not committed to winning. Protests, public denunciations, and debates continued. Sit-ins and demonstrations were held in front of government facilities as well as on college and university campuses across the country. This was the era of free speech forums in which people would stand up in public places to promote their causes, to give their perspectives and solutions, and/or to vent their frustrations.

INFLUENCES ON MY PREACHING

My journey through the turbulent 1960s deeply affected me. What I saw, experienced, and especially the words that I heard, in no small way shaped who I am today and in many ways influenced how I approach what I've been doing for more than thirty-seven years. On a Tuesday evening in February, 1966, at the age of sixteen, I preached my first sermon, and I've been preaching ever since.

I began preaching in a cultural context in which clear, strong speaking was the order of the day. The culture was concerned with questions of truth and "truth claims." We wanted to know who was right, who was wrong, what was right, what was wrong—and how you could know that what you believed and said was true. Alignment to what a person perceived to be true was more important than what a person felt about truth. This created in me an appetite and appreciation for truth. Although I did not know what the term *expository preaching* meant, from the very beginning there was a passion in me to know and understand what God's "truth book," the Bible, was all about and then to clearly and convincingly communicate the Word of God to people and the issues we face.

What all of this means in terms of my preaching style is that I tend to come across with a bit of a prophetic edge—not in the sense of foretelling the future but with an emphasis on a strong declaration of truth. God has something to say about how we live our lives and what he wants to do with our lives. Whether or not our culture wants to hear what God has to say in the final analysis is irrelevant. Our culture and our world cannot make it without a word from God!

> I began preaching in a cultural context in which clear, strong speaking was the order of the day.

But there's another, more significant contributing factor to my approach and philosophy of preaching that is deeply rooted in my spiritual pilgrimage. I was almost fourteen when I gave my life to Jesus Christ. From the very beginning of my spiritual journey, I was influenced by great biblical preaching. My pastor, the Rev. Burton C. Cathie, not only had supreme confidence in the power of the Word of God to change lives, but Sunday after Sunday he preached messages anchored in an explanation of the Scriptures. Burton Cathie preached the way he believed—that God uses his Word to change lives. I was also influenced by gifted preachers like Dr. Benjamin F. Reid and Dr. Samuel G. Hines who often came to preach at our church during my teen years. They were powerful, articulate preachers who were committed to the authority of the Scriptures and preached with a sense of humble, holy confidence that God was going to work in the lives of those who heard their messages.

> from the very beginning of my spiritual journey, I was influenced by great biblical preaching.

At that time Dr. Stephen Olford was the pastor of Calvary Baptist Church in New York City. Almost every Sunday morning before I went to church, I listened to him on the radio. His clear, strong, compelling expositions of the Word of God created in me a passion and thirst for the Scriptures which has yet to be quenched! On more than one occasion after listening to Dr. Olford, I can recall praying, "God, if I ever preach, I want to preach like this man." Looking back, it wasn't that I just wanted to be like Stephen Olford, Burton Cathie, Benjamin Reid, or Samuel Hines. No, I was attracted to something deeper; I wanted to honor God's Word in the same way they did.

But there's more. When I heard these men, and others like them, preach, God worked in my life. Many of the significant decisions I have made and the important changes in my life have come in response to the clear proclamation of the Word of God. I gave my life to Christ in response to a message my pastor preached. God has convicted me of sin as I've listened to the proclamation of the Word of God. God has many times answered questions that have troubled me as I heard the Word of God. God has clarified direction, given me solutions to problems, and encouraged my heart through the preached Word. My life has been and continues to be transformed through the preaching of the Word of God.

The point of preaching is the transformation of lives. There's no other reason for preaching. Life-change is the goal of all ministry, especially the preaching moment. The point of preaching is not to entertain or to impress an audience with our oratory, communication abilities, or knowledge. Let me say it again: The point of preaching is the transformation of lives. *Preaching is a word from God for the people at a moment in history.* When we stand to preach, we must be filled with a holy confidence that God has something to say to the people, and he is going to change lives because of the message he has given to us. It follows then that we must never stand before any group of people with a Bible in our hands and not expect change!

What I'm talking about is not simply the product of my exposure and experiences or my personal preference for a particular style of preaching. This conclusion—that the point of preaching is the transformation of lives—emerges from and is mandated by the Scriptures. In other words, there's a biblical basis and framework for this perspective on preaching.

I want to point to four passages that give us the biblical context and guide us in preaching for transformation. These texts come from the pen of the Apostle Paul, whose entire life and ministry were dedicated to the proclamation of the Word of God.

First Corinthians 1:18-25 tells us that preaching is God's sanctioned *method* for the transformation of lives. In these verses Paul uses the words *foolish* or *foolishness* five times. The message is that from a human perspective preaching is a very silly, foolish thing to do. Think about it. Somebody stands up in front of a group of people that he may not even know and gives a "speech" based on an ancient book. People actually listen, and some of their lives are changed. Granted, it's not the preaching that changes lives, it's the Spirit working through the message that produces change.

Yet, preaching is the God-sanctioned method and means by which the message is given. God's special power is manifested through his message and his unique favor is on the *proclamation* of that message. Look closely at 1 Corinthians 1:21, "For since in the wisdom of God the world through its wisdom did not come to know God, God was well-pleased through the *foolishness of the message preached to save those who believe"* (New American Standard Bible, italics added).

In recent times preaching has fallen out of favor. This is due in part to the fact that we are living in a culture that withdraws from a voice of authority. We don't like to be told what to do or that how we're living may be wrong. Now I wouldn't argue that there are many creative ways to communicate our message, but it's not in our hands to determine that preaching needs to be placed on the shelf for something "better." This passage underscores that preaching may look stupid and foolish to an unbelieving world, but it's the method through which God himself has chosen to make his wisdom known and to transform lives.

GOD'S MANDATE FOR TRANSFOR- MATION

This leads to the second biblical consideration. Preaching is the God-sanctioned *mandate* for the transformation of lives. When the Apostle Paul was facing death, he wrote a letter to his young disciple Timothy. Second Timothy 4:1-4 is one of the most tender, moving sections in the Scriptures. Paul is giving his son in the ministry a final reminder of the focal point of his ministry. I can only imagine the emotion that Paul must have felt as he penned these words to a younger man who would take up his mantle and advance the cause of Christ. Read the passionate, strong parting challenge Paul gives to Timothy:

> I solemnly charge you in the presence of God and of Christ Jesus, who is to judge the living and the dead, and by His appearing and His kingdom: *preach the word;* be ready in season and out of season; reprove, rebuke, exhort, with great patience and instruction. For the time will come when they will not endure sound doctrine; but wanting to have their ears tickled, they will accumulate for themselves teachers in accordance to their own desires; and will turn away their ears from the truth, and will turn aside to myths" (2 Timothy 4:1-4, NASB, italics added).

The principle that Paul wanted to burn into the soul of Timothy is that preaching is not to be determined or influenced by the "climate" and demands of people. Paul gave this charge under the authority and inspiration of the Holy Spirit. This is not just good advice; this charge is a divine mandate. And this mandate is for all of us who have the God-given assignment to preach. We're held accountable to a holy, sovereign

God ("...in the presence of God and of Christ Jesus, who is to judge the living and the dead...") for the faithful proclamation of the Word of God. No matter what's happening around us, we must preach. We're under the mandate to preach. Preaching is not a profession; it's a sacred assignment ordered by God to deliver a message, even when people don't want to hear it. God uses the faithful execution of this assignment to change lives for eternity!

GOD'S AUTHORITY FOR TRANSFORMATION

Preaching transforms lives. This is not to say that somehow the preacher has a "deeper" dimension of God or that he's in a "spiritually elite" category in God's eyes. The authority comes from the God-given message that we proclaim and *how* that message is preached. In 2 Corinthians 2:17, the Apostle Paul gives us the elements of the kind of preaching that evidence divine authority. Look at these words: "For we are not like many, peddling the word of God, but as from sincerity, but as from God, we speak in Christ in the sight of God." There are at least three elements mentioned in this text. These three elements must be present in our preaching if our preaching is to be characterized by divine authority.

• *Integrity.* First, when we preach, we must guard the integrity of the message. The word *peddling* in this verse comes from a Greek word that was often used of winemakers who deceived their customers. They would dilute the wine and pass it off as if it were 100 percent pure. If the scam went undetected, they could sell a lot of wine and turn a pretty good profit. They obviously didn't care that the integrity of their product had been violated. Paul's point is that we should not be "gospel hustlers" who are more concerned about what our audience wants to hear or what we want and don't want to tell them. Certainly we should be aware of who is in our audience and how we need to communicate so that we're heard, but we must never tamper with or change in any way the truth of his word to "sell" the message. Once we do, then God has left the building!

• *Sincerity.* Second, we must preach with utter sincerity. The expression "but as from sincerity" suggests that there is no room for pretense in the proclamation of the Word. God expects his messengers to be genuine to the core. The word *sincere* was sometimes used to describe Greek orators who would stand in public places and give passionate, eloquent speeches. People would throw money at them in appreciation of their presentations. It didn't take these orators long to realize that the better the speech the more money they made. They started out sincere, but many of them became disingenuous; they were orators who became actors. Unfortunately, this is true of too many preachers today who are using their gifts of persuasion to promote themselves and to line their pockets. It's an almost irresistible temptation to play to the audience. But if we're going to preach for transformation, then we must guard the sincerity of our hearts and preach with a genuine burden for the people—and mean every word we say.

• *Authenticity.* Third, we must preach with authenticity. This means that what we say must carry the "force of the original." Look at this line again: "but as from God, we speak in Christ in the sight of God." This is a sober reminder that when we preach we're not just giving a Christian speech; we're giving a message from God for the people. Our real audience is none other than God himself. When we stand in that preaching moment, a sense of holy fear should come over us. We're not just standing in front of an audience. We're preaching in the very presence of almighty God, and we're delivering the message that he has entrusted to us for that moment in history. This is the reason I'm committed to expository preaching. It's the Word of God that carries with it the force of the original. And the transforming power of God is present when we honor what he has said in his Word by faithfully preaching it!

| OUR APPROACH TO THE TASK | The final biblical consideration is found in 1 Corinthians 2:1-5. Our *approach* to preaching has a lot to do with whether or not lives will be changed. I love this passage because Paul outlines how he approached |

the proclamation of the gospel message when he came to the city of Corinth. Look at these words: "And when I came to you, brethren, I did not come with superiority of speech or of wisdom, proclaiming to you the testimony of God. For I determined to know nothing among you except Jesus Christ, and Him crucified. And I was with you in weakness and in fear and in much trembling, and my message and my preaching were not in persuasive words of wisdom, but in demonstration of the Spirit and of power, so that your faith would not rest on the wisdom of men, but on the power of God" (NASB).

Incredible words! Our approach to preaching should focus on the "testimony of God," should be Christ-centered, should acknowledge our inadequacy ("weakness," "fear," "trembling"), should be Spirit-empowered, and should point our hearers to a faith that rests "on the power of God."

The great expectation when we preach is that God is up to something, and he's going to use us for the transformation of lives and the accomplishment of his divine purposes for now and for eternity.

A LIFE THAT CAN PREACH

Over the long haul, our effectiveness as preachers will come out of the integrity and holiness of our walk with the Lord. In this sense, we should have lives that can preach. We must not only preach a message; we must aspire to *be* the message that we are preaching. I'm not suggesting that as preachers we're perfect models of everything we preach. No—we, too, are sinners saved by grace, and we struggle with sin and temptation just as everybody else. But as spiritual leaders, we are called to be examples, models for others to follow (1 Timothy 3:1-7; Titus 1:5-9).

God wants his message given through a life he can use. "Therefore, if a man cleanses himself from these things, he will be a vessel of honor, sanctified, useful to the Master, prepared for every good work" (2 Timothy 2:21, NASB). We must be deliberate and aggressive in working on areas of weakness and sin in our lives (1 Timothy 4:15-16). God is not playing games. When we don't deal with sin, he will disqualify us from ministry (1Corinthians 9:27).

> we must not only preach a message; we must aspire to be the message that we are preaching.

The heart cry of every preacher should be, "I want my life to tell the truth about what I'm preaching." Oh, how we confuse giftedness with godliness! Just because a person has a platform and can impress an audience with eloquence and even biblical insight doesn't necessarily mean that there's Christlike character behind the words. We should spend more time and attention cultivating intimacy with God and purity in our relationship with him than on the development of our gifts. If we do this, then when we stand to preach, we'll preach out of the overflow of hearts that are passionately in love with the Savior and lives that are clean.

My son, Bryan, and I, although preaching in different eras and different ways, both rest on one primary realization—preaching is a transformational process. I understand that needs and styles will differ with each generation of preachers. But each generation of preachers must realize that God uses preaching to transform people. Bryan's chapter will demonstrate that preaching for transformation connects with people of all ages and all backgrounds.

Crawford W. Loritts Jr. (http://www.livingalegacy.org/bio.htm) is associate director with U.S. Ministries for Campus Crusade for Christ and host of the daily radio program *Living a Legacy,* which is heard nationwide on the Moody Broadcasting network. He is the founder of Legacy, a ministry dedicated to rebuilding and restoring urban families. He is the author of four books including *Lessons From a Life Coach: You Are Created to Make a Difference* and *A Passionate Commitment: Recapturing Your Sense of Purpose.*

chapter eight

PREACHING FOR TRANSFORMATION, PART 2

BY Bryan Crawford Loritts

I love great preaching. From an early age, I had a great affinity for it. I guess the reason for this is because I grew up in the church, the son of a preacher. In fact, I'm the son of a great preacher!

As a family, we would travel around a lot to hear dad preach. And while I always loved hearing my father, I especially loved it when he preached in African-American settings (funny, we would always get on him about toning it down in white churches, and now I find myself having to tone it down!). Dad would get going, and the crowd would be talking back to him. Folks would fall out on the floor or jump over a few pews. And there I was, normally on the front row, rocking back and forth, being visited by that unique tingling in my spine that only came when I heard great preaching. That tingling would visit me when I heard men like A. Louis Patterson, Tony Evans, E.K. Bailey, Kenneth Ulmer, and my dad. In fact, I remember once being so moved by my dad's preaching that I got up from my seat and stood right by him, grabbing his leg with one hand and sucking my thumb with the other. (Whenever I tell this story to others, they always ask, "What did your father do?" Well, he just kept on preaching!)

While I've heard a lot of great preaching, I've heard some pretty bad preaching as well. Some messages left me offended and at times even angry. Once I was in church nodding off in the back (around the age of fourteen) during a bad sermon. This particular church had the cushioned pews with the wood trim on top that served as an uncomfortable head-rest (something tells me this was by design). As I was nodding off, I could vaguely tell that my head was coming dangerously close to smacking the hard top of the pew. But the temperature was too hot and the sermon too bad for me to come to my senses. All of a sudden, I heard a thunderous whack on the podium, and my head (along with several others) jerked to attention as the pastor screamed, "You can't love God and listen to rap music!" I wiped my eyes and quickly checked for drool. Then I tried to determine if what I thought I heard, I really heard.

> with one statement he killed their passsion.

I knew something was wrong when the church was dead quiet. This was one of those churches where there was normally a conversation taking place between the congregation and the pastor. The pastor would make a point, and the congregation would respond with a loud "Amen!" But not this time. No amens ascended from the congregation. Silence. Dead silence.

I nudged my friend next to me, wanting to know if my suspicions were true. Did the pastor really say what I thought he said? My friend didn't prove all that helpful, since he was doing the same thing I was. But later on I sadly discovered that the pastor did make that statement. I wonder what chapter he got that from? First Hesitations chapter seven I'm guessing. Yes, that's the passage where the apostle talks about the sin-fulness of following Christ and listening to rap music. Well, regardless of where he got it (certainly not the Bible), the damage was done. A group of boys my age who were just getting fired up about Christ were lis-tening, and one of the ways they chose to express their passion was through rap music. They used this medium with Christ-centered lyrics to spread the gospel. And the pastor just couldn't take it. With one state-ment he killed their passion. And to this day none of these men have made it back to church.

THE POWER OF PREACHING

That hot Sunday afternoon reaffirmed to me the potency of preaching. Right or wrong, someone who takes a position as God's representative, speaking into the lives of others, wields great power. Power to edify the body, moving people toward maturity in Christ. Or power to push them away.

Those words on that hot summer day proved to be a defining moment in my life. When I acknowledged God's call to preach the gospel just three years later, I remember making a conscious decision never to beat people up with my opinions or with the Bible. I decided to preach the Word of God with one great expectation: The announcement of God's truth coupled with the Spirit of God would produce transformation in the lives of the hearers! It's not my job to make people feel bad or even to change people. That's the Spirit's job; but he often chooses to do that through preaching.

I often wondered how that pastor could get away with making a statement as he did. I don't mean to justify what he said, but his insights came out of a very modern worldview. His approach to ministry, and especially preaching, was a very modern and linear approach. You know the approach—the pastor says it, so you do it! This approach lead to a very "in your face" style of preaching. In that time, people accepted it, and ironically that church grew.

Boy, times sure have changed…

Different era, same need

There's been a major shift in our culture. We've shifted from modernism to postmodernism. And postmodernism is morphing into whatever is next. The implications this has for us as preachers of the gospel in the twenty-first century are staggering! People living in a postmodern world have major hang-ups with absolute truth. Pluralism, relativism, and the new tolerance are evidences of this. What was widely assumed and accepted in modern culture is being questioned and picked apart in postmodern culture. Topics such as sexuality, morality, and faith have become volatile issues in our postmodern world. Yet the blessing of this is that people are willing to explore. They're willing to examine and draw conclusions. They're willing to take a journey, to process through the issues.

I discovered this when I led a postmodern ministry in Pasadena called The Warehouse. Over five hundred young adults were coming on Sunday nights; about twenty percent of them were not followers of Jesus Christ but were obviously seeking. I could always count on getting e-mails and telephone calls from them after a message on Sunday night. They wanted to talk more about some of the things I had presented from Scripture. Seldom were definitive conclusions drawn from our conversations. In fact, they would end with the person saying something to the effect of "You've given me a lot to think about. See you Sunday." And sure enough they would be back.

We didn't do an official altar call on Sunday nights, although we did give people a chance in our services to make a faith commitment to Christ. But we did have a lot of people coming to faith in God through his Son. How do I know this? People would come up to me and say something like "I've been coming here with my friend for the past six months. And afterward we would go out for coffee and discuss what you were talking about. Well, last week I finally decided this is what I want to do. I want to follow Christ!"

"people in a postmodern world are not persuaded to faith by reason as much as they are moved to faith by participation in god's earthly community."

Whenever I would hear statements like this, my heart would be overwhelmed with joy. My mind would be drawn back to Robert Webber's words in his book *Ancient-Future Faith,* "In a postmodern world the most effective witness...is the church that forms community and embodies the reality of the new society. People in a postmodern world are not persuaded to faith by reason as much as they are moved to faith by participation in God's earthly community."

Times have changed drastically from my father's day to mine. In a postmodern world, door-to-door evangelism that expects people in process to make immediate decisions detached from any community is not realistic (though by no means am I saying not to do it). Modern world assumptions like the inerrancy of Scripture, Jesus Christ being the only way, and the sinfulness of an "alternative lifestyle" (the very phrase should show you the shift in culture) are certainly not assumptions today. Yet as drastically different as the worlds that my father and I began preaching to are, the one thing that has not changed is the truth of Scripture, even though people's perceptions of it have. Because of this, great hope remains for the renovation of lives for the kingdom of God. This hope continues to fuel my passion for preaching because of the great expectation it offers—transformation!

TRANSCENDENT TRUTH AND RELEVANCE

I was invited not too long ago to speak to a group of college students from across the upper Midwest. After one of my sessions, a young man approached me, saying that his pastor had asked him to preach a message to his church on baptism, and he was obviously not thrilled by the topic. He wanted to know how he could make the doctrine of baptism relevant to his audience.

This young man's concern captures perfectly the heart of people in today's culture. They want to know what in the world does this passage, this message, have to do with me? Especially in a me-driven country like America, the question of relevance is a prevailing one. And nowhere is the question of relevance more asked and pondered than in the local church.

> The consumer christian of the twenty-first century is driven by the issue of relevance.

The consumer Christian of the twenty-first century is driven by the issue of relevance. What programs do you have for my kids? Does the pastor speak to me and my issues? How long does he speak? Is the service too long? Do you offer a service to fit my traditional or contemporary tastes? Is the worship led by an organ or a guitar? All these and more are questions centered around the driving concern of relevance. And unfortunately many churches have compromised the truth in their quest to be relevant.

I once had a pastor tell me that expository preaching is a thing of the past and that he's chosen to go topical because "that's where the people are." By no means do I want to argue over a method of presenting truth, but if what's driving your preaching is simply what the people want to hear, then there's a problem.

On the other hand, there are plenty of churches and pastors who have neglected the question of relevance and as a result have become irrelevant to the world and community that God has called them to serve. Some pastors are so driven to discover the "big idea" of the passage that they never take the time to show how this big idea relates to the woman whose husband has just left her.

So the question really becomes "Are truth and relevance mutually exclusive concepts?" The apostle Paul would say no:

> Though I am free and belong to no man, I make myself a slave to everyone, to win as many as possible. To the Jews I became like a Jew, to win the Jews. To those under the law I became like one under the law (though I myself am not under the law), so as to win those under the law. To those not having the law I became like one not having the law (though I am not free from God's law but am under Christ's law), so as to win

those not having the law. To the weak I became weak, to win the weak. I have become all things to all men so that by all possible means I might save some. I do all this for the sake of the gospel, that I may share in its blessings" (1 Corinthians 9:19-23).

Here the apostle helps us see that there's a place for relevance and there's a place for truth. In fact, to put it succinctly, Paul says the driving force behind his seeking to be relevant is the transcendent truth and power of the gospel. Paul goes on to explain that the gospel he presents centers around the person of Jesus Christ and his death and resurrection (1 Corinthians 15) and that the truth of the gospel has the dynamic power to transform lives (Romans 1:16). Paul so understood the power of the gospel that he boldly proclaimed to the Galatians, "But even if we or an angel from heaven should preach a gospel other than the one we preached to you, let him be eternally condemned!" (Galatians 1:8). Left to itself, the gospel has more than enough power to transform the lives of people for eternal purposes.

> The gospel is supernatural, requiring the work of God through his Spirit to regenerate the hearts of people.

William Barclay, in his book *Introducing the Bible,* tells a moving story that shows the power of the gospel:

> One of the most famous Bible stories in the world is the story of Tockichi Ishii. Ishii was a Japanese criminal with a unique record of savage murder. He was a man of fiendish brutality, pitiless as a tiger. He had callously murdered men and women and even little children. He was captured and condemned and he was in prison awaiting execution. He was visited by two Canadian women. They could make no impression on him; he would not even speak or answer; he simply glowered at them like a wild beast. In the end they had to go, but they left a Bible with him. For some reason Ishii began to read the book, and, when he started, he could not stop. He read on until he came to the story of the Cross. It was the saying of Jesus: "Father forgive them; they know not what they do," that broke him. "I stopped," he said. "I was stabbed to the heart, as if pierced by a five-inch nail. Shall I call it the love of Christ? Shall I call it his compassion? I do not know what to call it. I

only know that I believed, and the hardness of my heart was changed." When in the end the jailer came to lead him to the scaffold, instead of the surly, hardened, brutal, almost beastlike man he once had been, he went to death with a serene, smiling, gentle radiance, for Tockichi Ishii the murderer had been reborn by reading the word of God.

History is filled with countless examples of men and women whose lives were transformed when they were confronted with the gospel. Why? Because the gospel is supernatural, requiring the work of God through his Spirit to regenerate the hearts of people.

In 1 Corinthians 9:19-23, Paul was not only committed to proclaiming the truth of the gospel, but he was also committed to doing so in ways that connected with his hearers. Paul says, "To the Jews I became like a Jew." Study Paul's life, and you'll see that whenever he would plant a church among Jews, he would go to the Jews' turf, the synagogue, to reach them. With Gentiles he would go to the marketplace. He was radically committed to doing whatever it took (within biblical guidelines—see 1 Corinthians 9:21) to reach as many people as he could with the gospel.

PAUL, POWERPOINT, AND PREACHING

If Paul were here today, I'm convinced he would use PowerPoint, insert movie clips, maybe even shorten the message, and try to convey it in more inclusive terms. Why? Because Paul would be radically committed to using anything within biblical guidelines to reach postmodern culture. But with Paul, as it should be with us, relevance never drove the gospel. The gospel would always be his motivating force.

I believe passionately that Paul's words in 1 Corinthians 9:19-23 provide a framework for those of us who herald the gospel. The emphasis should never be on the presentation but on the gospel. We don't *preach* PowerPoint, video clips, or captivating stories. These are merely elements that help to season the gospel, the message. The goal is never to be an effective communicator but an effective preacher. A communicator is one who has so emphasized relevance and the techniques that the message has taken a backseat. A preacher is one who is obsessed first and foremost with the timeless, transforming power of the gospel. While he does seek to bridge the Bible to today's culture, this does not appear first in his order of priorities.

When we as preachers readjust our priorities so what really matters—the gospel—comes first, we may become less popular. Some people may leave our churches. And the invitations to speak may begin to dwindle.

Several years ago I began a policy of not looking at evaluations that people send me from the groups that I've spoken to. I made that decision after I received some evaluations from a Christian university I had visited. The morning I gave my last message, I remember wrestling with God in prayer over what to share, and I sensed heavily that God wanted me to preach a message on holiness (not a real popular topic). Convinced that this was the direction God was leading and having adequately prepared, I presented this timeless message on holiness from Isaiah 6. No one jumped over any pews, ran around the building, or gave any rousing "amens!" There was just silence.

> If Jesus was rejected because of the message he preached, then how much more should we expect negative evaluations and rejection.

A few weeks later the dean of the chapel sent me the evaluations. While there were many positive comments, my mind was quickly drawn to the negative ones. As I read through them I immediately found myself discouraged, wondering if I could have said what I said differently. At that moment an indescribable calmness came over me. It was as if God were saying, "Did you do what I wanted you to do? Well, keep moving. You will not always be accepted."

Men and women, in our line of work the issue is never one of acceptance. If Jesus was rejected because of the message he preached, then how much more should we expect negative evaluations and rejection. God has not called us to be effective communicators who strive to be embraced by all. God has called us to proclaim his gospel, his message. At times this will mean rejection because truth is convicting. May we give people the truth. God's truth! When we do this, we have the great expectation of transformation!

Bryan Loritts is currently the young adults pastor at Calvary Church in Charlotte, North Carolina. At Lake Avenue Church in Pasadena, California, Lorritts led the The Warehouse, a Gen-X ministry, from twenty-five people to more than five hundred people in less than two years. His ministry takes him across the country, speaking at churches, conferences, and retreats. Lorritts' ability to communicate the truths of Scripture in a relevant, uncompromising manner has helped to reach a generation entrenched in postmodernity.

chapter nine

PREACHING IN A CONVERSATIONAL COMMUNITY

BY DOUG BANISTER

One steamy June night in the summer of 2001, I left the kibbutz where I was staying on the Sea of Galilee and took a walk along the beach. The modern street lights of ancient Tiberias flickering across the lake were the only reminder that two thousand years had passed since Jesus had walked these shores himself.

I'm not a very mystical person. God usually speaks to me in his still, small voice. This night, however was different. Perhaps it was the cumulative effect of three dusty weeks wandering the holy places of Israel. Perhaps it was the magic of ancient winds sweeping down from the Golan Heights, bearing in their breezes the secrets of sacred pasts. Perhaps it was the need I had for a simple encounter with Jesus after many hours in the classroom and in the books. Whatever the cause, Jesus joined me on my walk that windy night. Or perhaps I joined him. Two millenniums slipped beneath the dark waves, and I found myself half imagining, half seeing a scene from the gospel of Mark: "As Jesus walked beside the Sea of Galilee, he saw Simon and his brother Andrew casting a net into the lake, for they were fishermen. 'Come, follow me,' Jesus said" (Mark 1:16-17a).

I sensed Jesus saying to me, "This is what it means to be a Christian. This is what it means to be a part of my church."

Then the encounter was over, and I was alone again on the beach.

A CONVER-SATIONAL COMMUNITY

I've thought about that simple vision of Jesus inviting Simon and Andrew to follow him many times since that night. When you boil it all down, being a Christian is following Jesus Christ. The church is a community of people who have chosen to follow Jesus Christ together. Jesus' first act was forming a community. "Jesus went up on a mountainside and called to him those he wanted..." Mark wrote. "He appointed twelve...that they might be with him" (Mark 3:13-14a).

The community would "be with him" in intimate, conversational relationship for three wonderful, terrifying years. They would rarely be apart. Jesus, the master teacher, would use every conceivable opportunity to shape them into a community. He taught them. He corrected them. He warned them. He listened to their questions. He challenged them. He protected them. Most of all, he guided them.

When the original twelve disciples said yes to Jesus, they also said yes to life in a conversational community. They learned to hang on every word their master spoke. Jesus, whom one of the disciples would later describe as "the Word" (John 1:1-14), was in continual conversation with his community.

The final hours of Jesus' life on earth find him, not surprisingly, in conversation with his community. It's Thursday night. The streets of Jerusalem are overflowing with dusty pilgrims arriving to celebrate Passover. The joyous sounds of festival, of laughter and greetings and preparation, fill the street outside the upper room where the community sits. The mood inside is not joyous. Jesus is somber as he prepares them for his death. The community's Passover dinner is a quiet one this year.

> when the original twelve disciples said yes to Jesus, they also said yes to life in a conversational community.

Jesus comforts them with a promise of continued conversation. "I will not leave you as orphans," he begins, noting the fear in their eyes (John 14:18a). "The Counselor, the Holy Spirit, whom the Father will send in my name, will teach you all things and will remind you of everything I have said to you" (John 14:26). He spends a few moments preparing them for what is to come and then returns to his comforting promise of continued conversation with the community. "But when he, the Spirit of truth, comes," Jesus says gently, "he will guide you into all truth...The Spirit will take from what is mine and make it known to you" (John 16:13-15).

Jesus is crucified. He rises from the dead. And then he calls together the community for a conversation. They meet on a favorite hillside in Galilee where they've talked many times before. Jesus instructs the community to go into all the world and invite others to become his followers, adding, "And surely *I am with you always,* to the very end of the age" (Matthew 28:20b, italics added). The conversation will continue.

Forty days pass. Jesus gathers the community together on the Mount of Olives, just outside of Jerusalem. He gives them their mission one final time before returning to heaven, commanding them to stay put until he sends them the gift of the Holy Spirit. They wait. Jesus pours out his promised Holy Spirit on the day of Pentecost. The Spirit comes. And the conversation continues.

CONTINUING THE CONVERSATION THROUGH PREACHING

The primary way Jesus continues his conversation with the community is through preaching. The first post-Pentecost event in the community was Peter's sermon. Peter makes it clear that his sermon is more than mere oratory. Jesus is not dead. He is alive and eager to speak to his church. "God has raised this Jesus to life!" Peter excitedly tells the crowd (see Acts 2:24). "He has received from the Father the promised Holy Spirit and has poured out what you now see and hear" (Acts 2:33b). Peter, preaching the church's first sermon, is a mouthpiece for the Holy Spirit.

Those who respond to the sermon gather together into new communities. Luke tells us that they "devoted themselves to the apostle's teaching" (Acts 2:42a). The early church was devoted to the teaching of the Word of God because that was where they heard the voice of Christ.

JESUS ACTIVELY LEADS HIS CHURCH TODAY

Jesus is the "head over...the church, which is his body" (Ephesians 1:22b-23a). The medical literature of Paul's day described the head as the command center for the body. The head leads, the body follows. The head and body are continually in an ongoing conversation with one another as the body responds to the head's initiatives. "The organic relationship between head and body suggests the vital union between Christ and the church," observes New Testament scholar F.F. Bruce. Together Christ and his church share "a common life, which is his own risen life communicated to his people."[1]

Conversation is a vital part of every intimate relationship. Christ deepens his vital union with his church by conversing with her through the proclamation of the Word. This is why Christ, after rising from the dead and ascending into heaven, gave gifted teachers to the church to help her mature (see Ephesians 4:11-12). Jesus is the head of his church. He actively carries on his conversation with his church through preaching and teaching the Word.

THE PASTOR AS MESSENGER

The Apostle John's vision on the island of Patmos provides an illustration of how Christ speaks into a community. In John's vision, Jesus writes a letter to seven different churches. He has a special word for each of them, uniquely tailored to each specific circumstance. Each message is given to "the angel" of the particular church. The word translated *angel* is *aggelos,* often used for human messengers in Greek literature. Many commentators understand *the angel* to be the human messenger called to bring Christ's word to the congregation. "The messengers were probably the pastors of these churches," concludes John Walvoord.[2] Jesus brings a fresh word to the pastor. The pastor brings the word of Jesus to the church. The pastor is a messenger, a channel through which Jesus converses with the community.

Significantly, each church receives a different word. The pastor's job is not merely teaching the Word of God to the church, as if it were a seminary class studying the Bible for a final exam. The pastor must bring a fresh, living word to his or her flock. Christ is not retired as the leader of his church. He's the active leader, and he has a specific word for each congregation. The primary way he wants to bring that word is through his messenger; the pastor-teacher (or team of teachers) who brings the word to the flock each week.

> christ is not retired as the leader of his church. He's the active leader, and he has a specific word for each congregation.

Christian theology understands the Word of God three different ways.

- Jesus is the living Word of God.

- The Bible is the written Word of God.

- Preaching is the proclamation of the Word of God.

When a man or woman preaches the Word of God to a congregation, all three uses come together. The preached word is from the written Word and reveals the living Word, Jesus Christ. Jesus speaks to his community through the sermon.

John Calvin went so far as to say that preachers are "the very mouth of God." The Roman Catholic writer and monk Thomas Merton described the preached word as an encounter with the living Christ.[3] Shortly after his resurrection, Jesus joined two of his discouraged disciples on the Emmaus Road and taught them from Scripture. "And beginning with Moses and all the Prophets, he explained to them what was said in all the Scriptures concerning *himself*" (Luke 24:27, italics added). The preached word reveals Jesus. "The words I have spoken to you are spirit and they are life," Jesus promised (John 6:63b). Our sermons should be the words Jesus speaks to us. These kinds of sermons bring life. The cry of the prophets to ancient Israel was "Come here and listen to the words of the Lord your God" (Joshua 3:9). This is the preacher's invitation as well.

MORE THAN
A LECTURE

Preaching in the conversational community is more than a lecture about an ancient sacred text. The community gathers expectantly, anticipating a fresh word from Christ shared through the preacher. The text comes alive by the Spirit and speaks powerfully into the community. The preacher works hard to explain what the Bible passage originally meant and works equally hard to listen to what the Spirit of Jesus wants to say to the community today through the passage.

Because the demands of pastoring a twenty-first century church are so great, many pastors take shortcuts in their sermon preparation. Some download their sermons from the Internet or subscribe to mail-order sermon services. Others pull out old sermons they preached years before. Studying how another preacher has handled a text is a very valuable tool in sermon preparation. Looking at old notes is not a bad idea. But taking someone else's sermon or pulling out one of your old ones and preaching it, violates the principle of Christ's active headship over his church. Jesus Christ wants to say something *now* to your congregation. Old words just won't do.

When a preacher opens the Bible and begins to speak, "people must hear more than what the Book says," wrote Watchman Nee. "They must hear the current voice of God."[4] Nee is referring to more than good, practical applications. He's describing a kind of preaching in which Jesus speaks through the text into the specific needs of the community. There is a "nowness" to this kind of preaching that leaves the congregation breathless. The congregation sits quietly, stunned. Jesus Christ has spoken to it. It will never be the same.

> Jesus christ wants to say something now to your congregation. old words just won't do.

HEARING AND SHARING THE FRESH WORD OF CHRIST

Many well-crafted sermons, however, still lack the *nowness* of Christ's current voice. We'd be wise to listen carefully to what an accomplished preacher told his students a generation ago:

"What is the Word of God? It is what God is speaking today, not just what He has once spoken. Once he spoke; and so we have the past Word of God. Now, though, we need him to breathe anew on his former Word."[5]

I stopped by an art store to browse one afternoon while traveling in another city. One particular painting caught my eye. The painting was a winter landscape set in the West. Muscular brown horses peered out from behind birch trees clustered tightly together in a snow-covered wood. Yet there was more to the painting than I was seeing—it had a scent of mystery about it. The store clerk eventually came and asked me what I saw.

"It's a painting of horses among birch trees in the woods," I said.

"Look again," she told me.

I did, and still saw nothing.

"Don't you see the Indians?" she asked.

Suddenly my eyes were opened and I could see a dozen Indians hiding behind the trees. It took the help of the clerk to make me aware of the reality hidden in the painting.

Many sermons present the trees but miss the Indians. We get the exegesis right, nail an illustration or two, and give some great applications. We don't take the time, or have the capacity, to see everything Christ wants to reveal to us in the passage.

It's not easy to prepare sermons like the ones I'm describing. I'm adding an additional step to the already demanding sermon preparation process. Many excellent resources already describe the fundamentals of basic sermon preparation. Let's assume that you have already mastered the basics of Homiletics 101. What can you do to hear and deliver the fresh word of Christ in your sermon?

■ *1. Increase your capacity for spiritual listening.* We cannot give away what we do not possess. If we're not able to hear the word of God personally, we won't be able to share the word of God when we preach. Every Christian is prewired to tune in to Christ's voice. Jesus describes himself as a good shepherd who speaks to his sheep. "He calls his own sheep by name…he goes on ahead of them, and his sheep follow him because they know his voice" (John 10:3b-4). It takes time to learn his voice, however. Some sheep know the shepherd's voice better than others. The shepherd of a congregation needs to sharpen his or her ability to hear the Chief Shepherd's voice.

> I find cultivating a conversational relationship with god perhaps the greatest challenge in my spiritual life.

Listening to Christ's voice is the heart of the spiritual life. Christians throughout the history of the church have practiced spiritual exercises to train the "inner ear" to hear the voice of the Spirit. These spiritual exercises include prayer, meditation, journaling, fasting, and solitude.

Many are returning to an ancient tradition to help them learn the sacred language of spiritual conversation. The tradition is called spiritual direction. A spiritual director is not a therapist or a discipler. A spiritual director helps you learn to listen to God's voice. I find cultivating a conversational relationship with God perhaps the greatest challenge in my spiritual life. It finally dawned on me that I've sought coaching in every other area of my life I felt needed developing. Why not seek a spiritual coach for my spiritual life? I presently have two spiritual directors. One lives in a city five hours away. We meet for an annual retreat and e-mail semiregularly. The other lives in my city. We meet monthly. These two men, one in his seventies, the other in his forties, teach me to listen to God's voice. They never tell me what to do. They help me discover what God wants me to do. They teach me to listen.

A preacher's number one gift to his congregation is his own spiritual life. We can't bring Christ's word to our people without being with Christ first. Jesus practiced an ebb and flow in his ministry. He spoke for God before the crowds and then retreated to be with God in the lonely places. "I have the sense that the secret of Jesus' ministry is hidden in the lonely place where he went to pray, early in the morning, long before dawn," writes Henri Nouwen. "In the lonely place Jesus finds the courage to…speak God's words and not his own."[6]

Preachers who want to speak God's words and not their own need to spend many hours in the lonely places.

TAKING ACTION

• **_Become familiar with spiritual direction._** Two good places to start are *The Practice of Spiritual Direction,* by William A. Barry and William J. Connolly, and *Holy Invitations,* by Jeanette A. Bakke. Susan Howatch's novels about the lives of Anglican pastors also introduce you to spiritual direction.

• **_Be comfortable with your own soul shape._** How you listen will be different from how others listen. Don't compare yourself with others.

• **_See your sermon preparation as a dimension of your own conversation with Christ._** Begin your preparation by journaling about where you are emotionally, physically, and spiritually. Invite Jesus to minister to you first in your sermon preparation.

■ *2. Approach the text expectantly.* One barrier to hearing the current voice of Christ is a mindset that doesn't expect Christ to still speak. A.W. Tozer describes this mindset in his famous book *The Pursuit of God:*

"A silent God suddenly began to speak in a book and when the book was finished lapsed into silence again forever...With notions like that in our heads, how can we believe? The facts are that God is not silent, has never been silent. It is the nature of God to speak."[7]

We need to approach our text with an expectant belief that Christ will speak to us through it for our congregation. Scripture stirs faith, so claim the promises of Scripture as you prepare. Ask God to speak to you and through you from the beginning of your sermon preparation.

TAKING ACTION

• *Reflect on your personal understanding of how God speaks.* Is there a gap between what you believe and what you practice? Are your beliefs changing? What do you really expect to happen when you sit down with a text?

• *Listen to believers from other traditions describe how God speaks to them.* What can you learn from them?

• *Think about your last sermon.* How expectant were you in your preparation? What hinders your expectancy? What increases your expectancy?

■ *3. Find a sacred space for sermon preparation.* God's people have often sought out sacred spaces to enhance their ability to know him and hear from him. Abraham met God in a wooded grove. Joshua met him in a tent outside of camp. Jesus often returned to a familiar olive grove to converse with God.

We are sensual people. God made us that way. The familiar sights and sounds and smells of our sacred places can help us center down and feel safe and open to God. For many years, I spent one day a week in a cabin by a quiet river preparing my sermon. I could feel my spirit becoming more quiet and attentive even as I drove onto the property.

Some pastors can find a sacred place in their offices. I have found my office often reminds me of the business of ministry— e-mails scream from the computer, phone messages demand to be returned. The cabin by the river became a sacred place, a lonely place, far from the pressures of ministry. I found that my day away became the spiritual center of my week. Sermon preparation became a time of spiritual renewal for me as well as a day of diligent work. Changing the scenery also helped remind me that my number one objective for the day was meeting with God.

TAKING ACTION

• *Recall the last time you really connected with God.* What was the setting like? Is there any way you can prepare your sermons in a similar setting?

• *Do you feel guilty about getting away from the office to spend time preparing?* Talk to your leadership team about this. Explain to them what it takes for you to prepare to hear the voice of God.

• *Does your sermon preparation process give you energy or drain energy from you?* How could you turn your sermon preparation time into a weekly spiritual retreat?

■ *4. Recruit a prayer team.* The great British preacher Charles Spurgeon once asked a visitor if he wanted to see his church's furnace. He took the man down a flight of stairs to a room situated just beneath Spurgeon's pulpit. "This is where the heat comes from," he said, opening the door. Several dozen prayer warriors were huddled together, interceding for the sermon Spurgeon was about to preach. Prayer was Spurgeon's furnace.

The kind of preaching that leads the community into a divine encounter with the living Christ is essentially spiritual. As important as the principles of homiletics are, the heat comes when the Spirit ignites a message. "My message and my preaching were not with wise and persuasive words," Paul reminds one audience, "but with a demonstration of the Spirit's power" (1 Corinthians 2:4).

As important as the principles of homiletics are, the heat comes when the spirit ignites a message.

Prayer downloads the power of the Spirit and releases this power into the preached word. "Pray also for me," Paul pleads, "that whenever I open my mouth, words may be given me so that I will fearlessly make known the mystery of the gospel" (Ephesians 6:19).

I'm in a ministry transition as I write this and am in the process of building these principles back into the rhythms of my new teaching ministry. The seasons in my preaching when I have experienced the most spiritual heat have always been grounded in a web of praying networks. Here's how prayer partnered with preaching worked in one particularly fruitful season of my ministry.

One network received weekly prayer requests via e-mail with specific information regarding the upcoming sermon.

A second network met with me on Friday for several hours. I shared with the prayer group what I sensed Jesus wanted to say to the church this week through the text. We worshipped for a season, waited on the Lord in silence, and then followed the Spirit's leading in prayer. Sometimes we prayed for a specific point of application. Sometimes we prayed for insight about where the sermon needed to go. Sometimes we prayed for an individual need in the prayer group that was surfaced by the text I was planning to preach on. The prayer meeting became a dry run for the worship service.

A third network, made up of the worship team and several intercessors, met on Saturday night before the worship team practice. We usually spent a half-hour praying over the sermon and the worship before practice began.

A fourth network met in a little room off to the side of the worship center and prayed through each worship service. During a season in which we were having four services, it was fascinating to watch the sermon develop throughout the day. The prayer team, the worship leader, and I learned to dance together. They shared key themes that emerged in prayer as I preached. The worship pastor and I shaped the service in response to what we sensed God was doing in our midst.

TAKING ACTION

• *Discern what your initial reaction is to the idea of a prayer team.* Does the idea appeal to you? Does the idea cause you anxiety? Why or why not?

• *Write down what you really believe about prayer.* What role should prayer play in your preaching if you really believe what you wrote?

• *Ask other pastors how they partner with their own prayer teams.*

■ *5. Listen to the body.* Many of us love to preach because we love the process of preparing sermons. We're readers. We're students. We spend way too much money on commentaries. We wear reading glasses. The seminary environment, modeled after a graduate school, attracts people like us. Most normal people don't want to spend three years studying Greek, Hebrew, church history, and systematic theology. We enjoy that kind of thing and even went in debt to do it. The seminary system rewards those who excel in this kind of environment.

This system runs the risk of turning out professors rather than preaching pastors. (My first year out of seminary, I actually graded some papers *in red ink* in a class I taught at a struggling young church!) But pastors are not professors, disseminating vast quantities of information to people taking notes in the pew. Pastors are preachers who long to bring the fresh word of Christ into the hurting hearts of their people every week. And we can't bring the fresh word without fresh experiences with our people.

Jesus said of his own ministry, "The Son can do nothing by himself; he can only do what he sees his Father doing" (John 5:19a). The fresh word of Christ comes when we discern what the Father is doing *in* our people. This only happens when we're *with* our people. A good shepherd knows the sheep.

Now sermons flow from broken hearts. Our sermons bring the current voice of God when we're immersed in the current needs of our people. Our preaching suffers when our days are filled with an endless blur of board meetings, long-range planning sessions, budget battles, and personnel hassles. You can't preach to a people you don't know.

TAKING ACTION

• **Look at your weekly planner.** How much time did you spend last week just being among your flock, listening to them, assessing needs? Does your answer surprise you?

• **Do you find yourself withdrawing from the flock over the years?** What painful experiences have caused this?

• **Do you listen to some of the flock more than others?** Do you have "hearing posts" set up across your congregation or just with those you're comfortable with?

• **Establish a listening group from a cross section of your body.** Listen to the group members before you preach to discern what needs they feel ought to be addressed in the sermon. Listen to them after you preach to hear real feedback—not the fake stuff you get on Sunday morning.

■ **6. Hold your notes loosely.** The church is not a Toastmasters Club. The sermon is not a speech. This means we must walk a delicate line between preparation and spontaneity. The nineteenth-century revival preacher Charles Finney never prepared before he walked into a pulpit, trusting in the Spirit to give him words to speak. Most of us are not so blessed. (The fact that Finney preached the same sermons to different audiences night after night also had something to do with his ability to preach without preparation.) Fresh, current-voice preaching does require careful preparation. I write down every word I want to say in my sermons and read them over many times before I preach.

> once the preparation is finished, we need to be able to throw the notes away if god so prompts us.

Once the preparation is finished, we need to be able to throw the notes away if God so prompts us. Admittedly, this can become an attention-getting gimmick: "Boy, God must really be at work today because the pastor's not using his notes." But there are times when Jesus may hijack your worship service and bring a word you hadn't prepared to give. He has the right to do this. After all, it's his church, not yours. Most of the time we won't throw our notes away, but we need to give the Spirit the liberty to redirect our words and lead us to places we hadn't planned to go.

TAKING ACTION

- *How do you feel about spontaneity in the pulpit?* Why do you feel this way?

- *How could you increase your receptivity to the Spirit's leading as you preach?*

- *Have you ever thrown your notes away?* What happened? Do you do this too often or not enough?

Good conversations are always reciprocal. Communication flows back and forth. Words are spoken, received, and responded to. We must also "complete the loop" in our conversations with God. It's not enough just to listen to a sermon. People need to respond.

Sermons without a time for response fit well with a professorial model. Professors don't really want a conversation. They want to get through their notes before the bell rings. Students may stay after class and ask questions if they wish.

People who've been addressed with a living word can't help but respond. Many churches build into their worship service a margin in which the congregation may respond to God's word in the sermon in a variety of ways.

■ **1. Silence.** Sometimes silence is the only response to make to a thundering word from God. When God preached his powerful word of rebuke to Job, the stunned man was so moved he couldn't speak. "I am unworthy—how can I reply to you?" Job muttered. "I put my hand over my mouth" (Job 40:4).

■ **2. Worship.** Sermons that exalt the glory of God, lift up the name of God, or celebrate the character of God often call for a response of worship. When a sermon reveals the beauty of God to us and we find ourselves blinded by the brightness of this vision, how can we close our Bibles and walk out the door? Preaching, especially preaching that brings the current voice of God, thrusts us into a divine encounter with this great God that touches our minds, hearts, and souls. Worship is the only fitting response.

■ **3. Testimony.** Churches often become scripted and controlled as they grow larger. Every minute is carefully planned. Every public word spoken is rehearsed, carefully edited, and then critiqued after its delivery. This is understandable. Who wants to waste the time of hundreds of people while somebody rambles through an unprepared remark?

Over-scripting a service can, however, quench a sense of dynamic presence. When everything is preplanned and there's no room for spirit-led spontaneity, the community loses a sense of sacred adventure. People no longer wake up wondering,

"What's going to happen in church this morning?" It scares me a little, but I like being in a church that lets the Spirit shape the morning.

The simple practice of standing up and telling the community what God has said to you in the service awakens faith in a speaking God. The testimonies I'm speaking of are different from the stories we have people share to illustrate a principle in our sermons. These are spontaneous testimonies in which the congregation is invited to share what God is saying to them *right now.*

This is risky. Even though the risk can be minimized with clear instructions, you never really know what a person is going to say when handed the microphone.

■ *4. Repentance.* "The word of God is living and active. Sharper than any double-edged sword, it penetrates even to dividing soul and spirit, joints and marrow; it judges the thoughts and attitudes of the heart" (Hebrews 4:12). When the sermon comes alive and probes the dark corners of human hearts, the community needs the opportunity to repent.

When Ezra gave one of the first expository sermons to the recently returned Jewish exiles, he "read from the Book of the Law of God, making it clear and giving the meaning so that the people could understand what was being read." Then we read, "...all the people had been weeping as they listened to the words of the Law" (Nehemiah 8:8-9b).

> when the sermon comes alive and probes the dark corners of human hearts, the community needs the opportunity to repent.

When Christ wants to cleanse the community through the preached word, the community better respond. Silence, especially in the face of a stern rebuke, is a poor way to complete the loop. A child who does not respond to his mother's correction has not been cleansed. A player who says nothing when his coach corrects him will be benched. When the current voice of Christ brought through the sermon calls the community to turn from its sins, it should have a chance to respond.

This may or may not look like a traditional altar call, a practice often frowned upon in some traditions. The altar call has a soiled reputation because it has been used mechanically, without a sense of what God is doing in the service. Every service does not need an altar call because God is not working the same way in every service. Standing up before the community and going to the altar as an expression of repentance reinforces internal commitments and encourages humility.

■ *5. Liturgy.* The word *liturgy* comes from two Greek words that mean "people" and "serving." The word has come to describe how God's people serve him in their worship by speaking and praying historic prayers and creeds.

God's people worshipped liturgically for a thousand years before Christ came, praying and singing the psalms to one another. The early church, birthed out of Judaism but immersed with the Holy Spirit, blended Spirit-led spontaneity with liturgical prayers.

> god's people worshipped liturgically for a thousand years before christ came, praying and singing the psalms to one another.

Over the centuries, churches tended to gravitate either toward liturgy or away from it. Today, however, churches are finding a marriage between liturgy and free worship that brings the strength of both forms into the worship service.

It can be hard to know how to respond when you're in the presence of God who has just stunned you with a personal word. This is when liturgy helps. The Lord's Prayer, the Apostles' Creed, and other liturgical prayers are comforting, familiar words. They have been in our spiritual family for thousands of years and provide a well-trod footpath back to the presence of God. Liturgy guides our response when words fail us.

■ *6. The Lord's Supper.* The preaching of the Word and the Lord's Supper were the centerpiece of the early church's worship (see Acts 2:42). Robert Webber, an historian of worship, observes that many younger Christians are moving towards evangelically alive liturgical churches because they encounter the living presence of Christ in the Lord's Supper. When we approach the table in faith we encounter "the healing power of Christ through the Eucharist."[8] Jesus, present by faith in the mystery of the Bread and the Cup, intensifies his presence in the community. We respond to his presence by partaking and encounter him in an even richer way.

■ **7. Acts of Consecration and Commissioning.** When Christ asks "will you" in the sermon, the community needs an opportunity to say answer "yes." This can be as simple as a moment of silence before a final prayer.

Some sermons invite specific groups in the congregation to say yes. A sermon on prayer might include a specific word to those in the congregation who feel God calling them to a ministry of intercession. A sermon on compassion might include a word for those in the body called to a ministry to the poor. A sermon on global missions might include an invitation to be part of a cross-cultural church-planting team.

> some sermons invite specific groups in the congregation to say yes.

If you feel a sermon is speaking to a select group of people in your congregation, it's important to let the people identify themselves as a part of that group. We invite these people forward to network them together and connect them with our church's equipping ministries. We also pray for them. Paul urged Timothy to "fan into flame the gift of God, which is in you through the laying on of my hands" (2 Timothy 1:6). We ask God to stir up the spiritual gifts present and fill people for the calling they're responding to.

PREACHING AS WRESTLING WITH GOD

Preaching that seeks and shares the current voice of God with the community is incredibly demanding but worth the effort. When Saturday night comes, and I still haven't fully heard what Jesus wants to say to his flock the next morning, I'm often reminded of Jacob's all-night wrestling match:

So Jacob was left alone, and a man wrestled with him till daybreak. When the man saw that he could not overpower him, he touched the socket of Jacob's hip so that his hip was wrenched as he wrestled with the man. Then the man said, "Let me go, for it is daybreak."

But Jacob replied, "I will not let you go unless you bless me" (Genesis 32:24-25).

May this be our prayer the night before we preach.

NOTES

1. F.F. Bruce, *The Epistles to the Colossians, to Philemon, and to the Ephesians* (Grand Rapids, MI: Wm. B. Eerdmans Publishing Company, 1984), 275.

2. John F. Walvoord, *The Revelation of Jesus Christ* (Chicago: Moody Press, 1966), 53.

3. Thomas Merton cited in M. Robert Mulholland Jr., *Shaped by the Word* (Nashville: The Upper Room, 1985), 40.

4. Watchman Nee, *The Ministry of God's Word* (New York: Christian Fellowship Publishers, Inc., 1971), 94.

5. Nee, *The Ministry of God's Word,* 85.

6. Henri J.M. Nouwen, *Out of Solitude* (Notre Dame, IN: Ave Maria Press, 1990), 14.

7. A.W. Tozer, *The Pursuit of God* (Camp Hill, PA: Christian Publications, Inc., 1982), 81.

8. Robert Webber, *Ancient-Future Faith* (Grand Rapids, MI: Baker Books, 1999), 111.

Doug Banister is the founding pastor of Fellowship Evangelical Free Church, in Knoxville, Tennessee. Doug is the author of *The Word and Power Church* and *The Sacred Quest*. Prior to helping start Fellowship Church in 1987, Doug had eight years of ministry leadership experience in other pastoral positions and the campus ministry of Campus Crusade for Christ.

chapter ten

PREACHING TO POSTMODERNS

BY RON MARTOIA

"Wow! what an experience! Ron, I've never had these kinds of things happen to me before. I feel so moved and touched. I really feel as if I'm moving closer to Jesus. I think you're right; it's only a matter of time."

—a thirty-something doctor who had been attending our biotech series titled "Informing Decisions."

"Ron, I'm so glad I found this place! I've just moved here from Tennessee and can't believe I've found a place that so moves me. I'm a songwriter, and I've never been in a service where the art, message, and music all just pierced my heart."

—a twenty-something, single mom during our recent "Greenhousing Your Kids" series.

These stories could be multiplied hundreds of times as people molded and shaped by our transitional era give expression to the "feel" of the weekend experiences we at Westwinds call Fusion. Their very words may suggest the biggest difference between the world of modernity and the current postmodern world. Notice that the words *experience* and *feel,* not *rational learning,* take center stage. In the words of author Robert Webber, "There has never been a major shift in culture without an observable shift in communication."[1] People today want to encounter the Divine, not simply learn abstract principles about the Divine. Many in the church today will only allow the latter to be classified as preaching, but…

> people today want to encounter the Divine, not simply learn abstract principles about the Divine.

Stories like the above lead me to believe that a chapter title like "Preaching to Postmoderns" deserves at least a quick shot at definitions. Such a title presumes there must be some difference between preaching to postmodern people and preaching to their modern counterparts. Using my modern seminary training, I could dive into the original languages, doing semantic, lexical, and contextual analysis of the words connected to *preaching.* However, I think there's no reason in an article like this to do so. Let's simply agree that *to preach* is to communicate the truth of God's Word in a way that the recipients can understand in their culture.

TALKING HEADS AND BEYOND

Of course, like all definitions, this one is freighted with meaning not superficially apparent. Nine out of ten readers will have a default setting at the outset that when the word *preaching* is used, it's referring to a talking head expounding a biblical text. The talking head usually speaks for twenty to fifty minutes depending on the tradition or context. But the talking-head model of preaching may in fact be more a product of the post-enlightenment modernist project than a biblical construct. In fact, the idea of a learned pulpiteer orating a well-designed message is probably more rooted in scholasticism than it is in the whole of the New Testament. In such a modernist mindset, a discussion about preaching is essentially a discussion about sermon construction. Witness the traditional training pipelines of seminary education, seminaries' obsession with homiletics classes (which I too endured), and the content of homiletics texts. Communicating God's truth is about how you prepare and deliver sermons.

For all our obsession with sermon construction, from opening hook to three well-transitioned points with a concluding application and requisite illustrations, we certainly have baptized a model that's strangely absent in the book from which we so ardently claim we extract our forms. Paul makes it quite clear (see 1 Corinthians 2:4-5)—and Jesus models the same—that communicating God's truth is not simply a verbal exercise but has an extensive experiential component. We'll return to this observation in a moment.

For many of us, Post Raisin Bran is the only *post,* other than the post office, we're that familiar with. We're uncomfortable reflecting on and defining *postmodern.* This word has been so flippantly thrown around with so many definitions that it has come to mean almost anything. When something can mean anything, it's simply another way of saying the word means nothing.

So when we say we're preaching to postmoderns, to whom do we claim to be speaking? Some conceive a division along generational lines: Immigrants, moderns, or boomers are those born before 1962. They see our world in analog categories and are products of modernism.[2] In simple terms this means moderns are more linear, single tasking, and rational. They use maps; they like stability and solidity. The dominant metaphors of their work life betray their love affair with the predictability of a world where stability and mechanics are revered. Modernists have common sayings like "Keep her firing on all eight cylinders," "Keep the machine well-oiled," "Keep your feet on solid ground," and "Are you firm on that?" Stability and firmness are so esteemed that liquid metaphors are typically negative: *wishy-washy* or *watered-down.*

> when something can mean anything, it's simply another way of saying the word means nothing.

Natives, busters, or Gen Xers are those born since 1962 and are part of the transitional flux that's moving us into a new emerging world. For precisely this reason, certain writers have suggested that the dominant metaphors of our time should be *liquidity* and *fluidity.*[3] We don't even have a name for this new world yet, so we're just calling it *after-modern* or *postmodern.* The truth is, today's church functions in a transitional age that I believe will usher in the next worldview we are currently calling postmodern.

While I think the generational distinctions are *generally* true, I'm not convinced they're always accurate. In the church I planted sixteen years ago, we have some sixty-year-olds that are more tuned in to and influenced by current culture than some of our twenty-something leaders. These older individuals are therefore more postmodern.

With all this in mind, let's make some observations on what we see and hear in our postmodern world: Our current transitional cultural context is more circular, loopy, and nonlinear than the culture of recent decades. People are more into compasses than maps because they're exploring new terrain. They perceive the world more as a living organism than a massive mechanical system. The dominant metaphors of their world are more fluid than stable. They surf—either the Web or the white water of cultural change. In short, they go with the flow.

PERCEIVING I have no intention of cataloging the vast array of changes going on in our culture; I simply want to note that an unmistakable change is happening, and its magnitude registers high on the Richter scale. Far beyond a simple divide along generational lines, the postmodern age is influencing all of us in one way or another. Arguably, the most powerful shift in our culture is from a world where information, reason, and the mind are the dominant tools of perceiving to a world where transformation, experience, and the heart are the ascendant avenues of taking in our surroundings. In this regard, our current context is more like the premodern world of the biblical text than the modern world where reason and science held dominant sway. To answer our original question of who are the postmoderns we're speaking to, we're speaking to those of any age who've imbibed, been molded by, or have adopted the underpinnings of this emerging new world.

IMAX
SURROUND
SOUND

In the Bible, God's communication to his people seems anything but a rational exercise in oration. Moses received his marching orders one day while minding his own business: Out of nowhere he had a live—better than high-definition TV—viewing of God's presence in a talking bush that was also on fire. Preaching? Moses confronted Egypt not with a full complement of homiletical tooling but with a number of get-your-attention experiential components that caused engagement far beyond a rational level. Plagues have a way of being very experiential.

Preaching? The children of Israel had an incredible experience of God before they had much rational understanding of God on Mount Sinai. God gave the Hebrew people the most ancient IMAX experience we have on record—full surround sound, lightning, earthquakes, smoke, and fire. So powerful was the immersive experiential assault that the children of Israel said, "Hey Mo, *you* go!" And that he did. Preaching?

THE PRIMACY OF EXPERIENCE

The point? Experience preceded rational understanding. Interaction with the Divine was followed by explanation of the Divine. The list of such experiences could go on and on throughout the Old and New Testaments. It seems as if our modernist culture has, in fact, reversed the polarity of these two. We are obsessed with filling minds with information in hopes that in the process a transformative experience will result. With the emergence of this transitional world we're in, we see a return to what is more premodern and preliterate. Experience seeks understanding. If these observations are true, and my context certainly bears this out as do numerous other colleagues of mine, then preaching to postmoderns has to move beyond the arena of message mechanics into the broader arena and art of experience design.

Such a move would potentially see the entire experience of a weekend service as "preaching." If preaching is communicating God's truth in a way that the recipients can understand, then other elements and dimensions of the weekend experiences we provide are potentially part of the preaching dynamic as well.

The primacy of experience is probably the biggest difference in the way moderns and postmoderns attain truth. Modern people expect to drink quietly from a fountain. Postmodern people prefer to slurp from the blast of a fire hydrant. The first is a pretty easy, simple, steady stream; the other is a bit more chaotic, overwhelming, and drenching. Everyone would agree that both put out life-giving water, but everyone would also agree that the experiences of both are oceans apart.

FISSURES AND FUSION

Carefully defining your goals for your weekend experience is critical. Each weekend we have sixty to seventy-five minutes, during which each moment provides an opportunity to create an environment where the truth of God's Word can be experienced by an inquirer or seasoned veteran Christ follower. We see each Fusion experience (Fusion is the name of our weekend services) as a moment collection. Each moment is designed to increase the possibility of people bumping into the presence of God and to lead them toward deeper connection with Jesus, where soul fissures can be healed and next steps of growth taken.

The only immutable part of our Fusion philosophy is that the truth of God's Word must be the central focus of each weekend experience. What we don't say in that Fusion philosophy is that the truth of God's Word must be delivered through a thirty-minute talking-head segment. In fact, in the last twelve months we have only had one Fusion with a single talking-head segment. We almost always have two or three short segments woven through the experience. They are not "the sermon." They are part of the whole experience.

> The only immutable part of our Fusion philosophy is that the truth of God's Word must be the central focus of each weekend experience.

Let's look carefully at designing the full experience as the primary way of communicating God's truth (preaching) in a way the culture (postmodern) understands. In the process we'll also explore the talking-head role and where it fits and flows in the overall experience.

One of the biggest shifts in our weekend experience design is the move from tightly focused, single-theme programming to a much more webbed interlocking of a major theme with several other smaller themes. Monothematic programming is a child of modernity. It's rational, linear, singular, and mechanical, and it assumes only certain abilities to process one thing at a time. How does a web of interlocking themes preach when compared to the one theme that is drilled every time you turn around? Here's another big shift in our culture. A computer analogy is apt.

DOS OR WINDOWS?

The move from the MS-DOS operating system, which allowed you to do one thing at a time, to the Windows operating system, which allows you to do multiple things simultaneously, is a good image of what we're talking about. In a Windows environment (and for you Mac-addicts the same applies), there's only one active window, while others can be open and even performing different operations in the background. If we're doing a parenting series, like our already-mentioned "Greenhousing Your Kids" series, having a monothematic approach excludes people without kids as well as empty nesters. But if the main theme is parenting with two sub-themes of creating ambience for our kids and learning about emotional intelligence so we can foster it in the kids around us, then all of a sudden this isn't just a parenting series. It becomes a series on how you (no matter what your age or kid status) create space for kids to flourish and how you can increase your EI quotient. There may, in fact, be two or three "by design" sub-themes that provide handles for those who may not connect as readily to the main theme. Multiple themes are just one of the multiples we could mention.

FROM MONOTHEMATIC TO POLYCHROMATIC

The movement from monothematic to polychromatic means the multiple layers, various textures, and differing colors thematically provide much more to hang onto and make the experience that much deeper. Again, such an experience is more like drinking from a fire hydrant than a drinking fountain, but a drinking fountain is pretty boring once you've tried a fire hydrant.

Concretely this means that at any given point in the experience, multiple things are going on. One screen may display digital art and a question for reflection. Another screen may be scrolling a piece of poetry. Both of these media pieces create a backdrop to a seven-minute talking-head segment with ambient music and lemon scent underneath it all. Does all of this preach? You bet it does.

Our recent biotech series started with a reading from Aldous Huxley's *Brave New World*. At the same time one screen was scrolling photos of Huxley with poignant quotes, another screen was showing excerpts of other portions of his writings germane to the biotech predictions he made. The whole time huge three-dimensional, suspended double helixes were lit with red and blue and surrounded by neon green binary code on three black twenty-foot walls. People from the analog age of modernity look at the multiple visual things going on and struggle with which one they're to engage and pay attention to. They're still living in a DOS era. Those from the transitional digital age look at the layers, the colors, the scent, and immerse themselves in the experience. They multitask through it and meet Jesus in it. They're hearing a message preached through the colorful medium of a Windows environment. The DOS world of the black screen with single lines of alphanumeric characters is simply too one-dimensional to hold the attention of or connect with the postmodern being.

WORD HAS GIVEN WAY TO IMAGE

The once dominant format of *word* has given way to the more evocative *image*. Word was the syntax and grammar of modernity; image and experience are the currency of postmodernity. If a picture's worth a thousand words, then video must be worth millions. The era of word was about linear, rational, deductive, extracted principles. The era of image is about metaphor, story, narrative, digital art, sculpture, painting, video.

In every weekend experience, we seek to have a metaphor, dominant image, or icon that communicates the theme for the day. Fusion this weekend was titled "Tattoo Faith." How do we make the image of God, his tattoo on our lives, clearly seen? A video life story of a gal who came to Christ at Westwinds shared her spiritual journey by walking us through her various tattoos. Each one represented some god, part of an ancient religion, or segment of her god-quest. Her search ended when she found total acceptance in Jesus and the God-shaped hole in her heart was filled. Preaching? Indeed. Authentic, real, genuine, and raw; this is the language of postmoderns who are sick of plastic, fake, artificial, and postured. The two brief talking-head segments were hard-hitting expositions from Colossians 3. Multiple screens with motion graphics, a video interview of a tattoo artist, and explanations of why this is so viral in our culture were also a part of the service.

> If a picture's worth a thousand words, then video must be worth millions.

THE VERBAL SIDE

For the reader who's still looking for guidance in the preparation of the postmodern talking-head segment, let's make some observations. In the postmodern audience, we have entered a post-seeker age. What does this mean? It does not mean that the seeker movement has not taught us a tremendous amount about how to reach people still looking for God. It does mean, however, that in typical postmodern form we're not speaking to either seekers or to Christ followers; we're speaking to and designing the experience for both. Modernity was about either/or. Postmodernity is about both/and. We must prepare talks that have multiple layers just like the Fusion experience must have multiple themes, multiple screens, and multiple textures. We have to speak to the fresh inquirer and the twenty-year veteran Christ follower.

In my preparation I engage a process called the "Lion-King Principle."[4] When some family friends went to the movie *The Lion King,* the father noticed that one scene provoked laughter from his five-year-old, but no one else in the family laughed. Another scene moved his nine-year-old, but no one else seemed moved. Certain family members found resonance with certain sections of the movie, but rarely did everyone find the same scenes moving, funny, or engaging. The entire movie had impact, but different portions moved different age groups and maturity levels at different times. *The Lion King* managed to engage a variety of ages simultaneously. The moviemakers had created layers of communication; communication came in word, image, color, and motion.

I love to use "Lion-King Principle" to explain what I've always called *layered preparation*. To this day I prepare portions of my weekend talks at a local mall, bar, or restaurant. The single mom with three kids in tow, walking down the middle of the mall, needs to be able to walk into my weekend talk and understand most of what I say. She needs to be able to receive something of practical value even if she has never set foot in a church and has no god-knowledge of any sort. I ask myself, "What would the twenty-eight-year-old guy blowing in after work to grab a cold one get if he were invited by a friend to Westwinds and heard my weekend talk?" These are the first-layer lenses I wear when I'm preparing.

NOAH WHO?

The first lens allows me to check three factors: *language, real,* and *functional*. The *language* factor is now much more natural than it was even five or six years ago, but it does take practice and awareness. I check on how much church culture and in-house, theological, or Christianese language have crept into my talk. The natives of the postmodern era are the most unchurched generation in recorded history; as a result, biblical ignorance is the norm. To talk about Jonah may not conjure images of a whale. To speak of Noah may more quickly bring to mind the last name Wyle, as in *ER* of television fame, than connect the listener with the word *ark. Abraham* is more quickly connected to the sixteenth president of the United States than the patriarch that's the forefather of the children of Israel. If that single mom walks in, does she need a dictionary for all the parochial terms or connections we automatically think of, or is everything transparent? I'm not speaking of dumbing down or using uninteresting vocabulary. I'm speaking about using words and terms like *Christology, studying the Word,* or *coming to Jesus,* about which my uninitiated single mom or young executive would be clueless.

The *real* factor could hardly be more important. The viral TV shows of *Survivor* and *Fear Factor* show this craving for the real and the raw. Postmoderns have radar that detects anything artificial, fake, plastic, or postured. They don't like image management in general and are especially allergic to it from the platforms of churches. As such, one of the big shifts we see in talk preparation is the movement away from illustrations that are dominantly historical to ones that are primarily personal. Listen to preaching from the modern era, and you're apt to get a history or current event lesson during many of the messages. The illustrations are functional, appropriate, interesting, and useful, but they disclose nothing about the speaker. Historical illustrations don't connect to the postmodern, who's more interested in seeing if this stuff works for the speaker than in hearing a tear-jerking Civil War story. Real, raw, genuine, and authentic are the modem connections postmoderns make.

Not long ago during a weekend talk, I shared how my wife was getting the mail when our unchurched neighbor was doing the same. As they struck up a conversation, Valerie mentioned something about the "blowout" we'd just had. Our neighbor looked totally shocked and said, "You guys fight, even with Ron doing what he does?" Of course, the congregation all laughed as I gave the details. But the power in the realness of this illustration came

> postmoderns have radar that detects anything artificial, fake, plastic, or postured.

home when several people mentioned the comfort they took in realizing that leaders, well-studied people, and even prayed-up pastors like Ron Martoia, have marital snags. These are the kinds of stories that build credibility and approachability.

TRUTH EMBODIMENT

The third area of this first lens helps me navigate the *functional* factor. Can that single mom take away anything that really works Monday morning? Is it biblical truth? Is it practical truth? Is it communicated in a way that helps her learn how she can better live the life that Jesus would live if he were in her body? We need to give embodied truth. Modernity specialized in abstract, principled extractions from the biblical texts; postmoderns must experience an incarnational message that lives in front of them as it's preached to them. Illustrations from real life aren't additional niceties that help postmoderns understand. Illustrations from real life *are* the message; they're enfleshed truth, not abstract propositions.

The "Lion-King Principle" applied means we'll attempt to create talks that will hit both the new inquirer and the veteran. We have no illusions that all parts of the talk will hit all parties. In fact, by design we will build into the talk certain portions, language, and illustrations for one specific group or another. At times both groups will be hit, but usually we will lean on the "Lion King Principle."

THE OTHER LENS

If the first lens for talk development is to view the average nonchurched inquirer as a potential listener, then the other lens is to view how my talk would hit the mature Christ follower of several years. The lens for Christ followers allows me to check for depth, resource brokering, and fresh-insights. Depth is key for the Christ follower. Once an inquirer has decided to live the life of Jesus, we want to help that person move deeper. So we must not only make sure our message is intelligible for the uninitiated, but we also must make sure that the growing and mature get something that helps them move forward with Christ. Of course, this may be the spot where the new inquirer may lose some clarity for a minute or two, but that's no problem; this part of the message doesn't need to connect in a transparent way.

Next steps are also important; this is where it becomes important to be a resource broker. Our postmodern age is marked by an avalanche of information. We want to help Christ followers know their next steps for personal growth and point them in the direction of articles, books, Web sites, and other online resources for those steps. Rare is the weekend talk where I don't mention resources, post Web sites or book covers on one of our media screens, or provide program inserts listing a compilation of resources. Part of our role is to keep the postmodern grounded and focused in the sea of constantly proliferating information. With nearly fifty thousand books a year published in the United States, not to mention Web sites and articles in magazines, knowing what information is worth pursuing is a tremendous gift to give someone.

The final thing I want to be sure to communicate is fresh insight. We need to be careful we're not merely trying to share innovative or novel insights for the "wow!" factor. But we want to help people make previously unseen or unclear connections. We want to make biblical observations that may require more reflection or study than the average person has time for. When these three factors are joined with the three factors from the inquirer lens, we're on our way to preparing a talk that speaks to both the new inquirer and the veteran Christ follower.

JUST ONE STEP CLOSER

What's our real outcome goal in these talks and experiences geared toward postmoderns? Quite simply our goal is to move them one step closer to Jesus. This is true of the inquirer and veteran alike. All of us are on a continuum that shows some distance between us and the ideal goal of living the life Jesus would live if he were in our bodies. The inquirer is well to the left on the continuum. What obstacles might we be able to remove or questions might we answer that would enable the inquirer to move one step closer to Jesus? What negative cycles might be disrupted or sin patterns broken that could bring the Christ follower into greater health and wholeness in Christ?

> part of our role is to keep the postmodern grounded and focused in the sea of constantly proliferating information.

The Christ follower is decidedly more to the right on the scale but still has lots of real estate to cover to become the very embodiment of Jesus. The Engle Scale[5] of the '70s was a continuum of a number of steps that charted the basic migration path from hostile non-Christian all the way to committed Christian, seeking to be like Christ. A new Engle Scale would be very helpful in charting the types of steps people take on their journeys and examining the barriers we need to remove as we seek to understand the process of someone becoming a follower of Christ.[6]

ENVIRONMENTAL ARCHITECTS

Preaching to postmoderns, then, is as much about experience design and ethos creation as it is about talk construction. We're not just talking heads; we're experience designers and architects of space and environment. Preaching in this age means we must examine our cultural context and determine how that context may change the methods, mediums, and syntax of our communication without changing the message we're compelled to share. Preaching in the postmodern era takes cultural exegesis just as seriously as biblical exegesis but does so with a goal of using image, metaphor, narrative, and multiple textures to communicate the truth of God's Word. There could hardly be a more exciting time to "preach" than in this transitional age we are calling postmodern.

NOTES

1. Robert E. Webber, *The Younger Evangelicals: Facing the Challenges of the New World* (Grand Rapids, MI: Baker Books, 2002), 61.

2. Immigrants and native reference credit goes to Leonard Sweet, *Carpe Mañana* (Grand Rapids, MI: Zondervan, 2001), 14.

3. Zygmunt Bauman, *Liquid Modernity* (Malden, Massachusetts: Blackwell Publishers, Inc., 2000), 1. From a secular perspective: William Berquist, *The Postmodern Organization: Mastering the Art of Irreversible Change* (San Francisco: Jossey-Bass Inc., Publishers, 1993), 9-10. From a Christian perspective: Leonard Sweet, *AquaChurch: Essential Leadership Arts for Piloting Your Church in Today's Fluid Culture* (Loveland, Colorado: Group Publishing, 1999), 24.

4. I am indebted to my friend Vince Beresford, who first used this illustration in describing what he observed about my weekend talks.

5. For the complete Engle Scale, see: www.cmf.org.uk/evang/conf/engscale.htm

6. I hope to finish shortly my twenty-first-century version of the '70s Engle Scale. The language and categories used then are now dated and unhelpful in light of our growing understandings of conversion and the largely relational rather than rational categories of the process.

Ron Martoia serves as lead pastor and transformational architect at Westwinds Church in Jackson, Michigan, a church he planted fourteen years ago. Westwinds is a leading church in the arts and in experiential worship. Ron is also the author of *Morph!: The Texture of Leadership for Tomorrow's Church* (Group Publishing, Inc., 2002).

chapter eleven

PREACHING DOWN UNDER

BY E. glenn wagner

"Apart from me you can do nothing."
—john 15:5b

"To me there is nothing more terrible for a preacher, than to be in a pulpit alone, without the conscious smile of god."[1]
—D. Martyn Lloyd-jones

In my twenty-five years of preaching, I have felt two things and have not been able to predict them. I have felt and known that my preaching has, at times, done little more than consume thirty or forty minutes of time. No power. No lasting change in the hearts of people. No spiritual victories. At times, the sermon itself had all the makings of "great" preaching—a gripping introduction, a creative outline, personal illustrations, and a call to response. And yet, when I preached it, it felt powerless. Many times I have felt as if I were trying to push a train with a piece of spaghetti, getting nowhere real fast.

On the other hand, I've also felt God's unique activity, his special presence at work, in the place I was preaching. It's that distinct sense that more is happening than just my delivering of words. God is choosing to accompany the preaching with his special touch or, in the words of C.H. Spurgeon, "the sacred anointing." D. Martyn Lloyd-Jones described it as sensing "the smile of God." It's when you feel as if Jesus Christ himself is doing the preaching, and you just happen to be the closest mouth to use.

> It's when you feel as if Jesus Christ himself is doing the preaching, and you just happen to be the closest mouth to use.

I felt God's "smile" just recently. It was a Sunday like every other Sunday. The worship was great, but it always is at Calvary Church. There was a lot of excitement in the room, but this too is normal. I had a great week in study and prayer over my message, but these are regular habits for me. In other words, as I reflect on this particular morning, I can't pinpoint anything extraordinary about it. But when I stood to preach, I quickly realized this was no ordinary Sunday. One of my staff pastors said that within fifteen seconds he realized that God was descending on us through the preached Word. Almost immediately I had a freedom and authority to communicate God's message that transcended my normal experience. There was a power welling up from inside my soul that broke through many of the normal barriers of human communication. Fearlessness, conviction, and urgency were coupled with love, brokenness, and humility.

I realized that God owned my heart and Calvary's heart that morning. It seemed as if God energized every word that I spoke. I could see, hear, and feel the effect on the congregation. They were with me not just physically but spiritually and emotionally. Many were visibly broken and moved. I was consumed with the testimony of God's work that morning. God showed up.

Once you experience God's smile in preaching, you dread not sensing it.

So how do you go about experiencing more often this power in preaching? Well, first, this is God's sovereign domain. You can't calculate when he can or should empower your preaching. God reserves the right to bless or not bless our preaching according to his will and purpose. Empowered preaching is not just the result of the right use of means. In other words, it's not just one plus one always equals two. God-empowered preaching is the result of being "down under" God, not just in our preaching but in our entire life.

GETTING DOWN UNDER GOD

When you realize that God is the pastor-teacher of your church and that you are merely his instrument, it changes everything. Getting under God is simply the process by which you acknowledge, pray, and model the fact that without God's special touch, your preaching is powerless. It's when you tangibly demonstrate that your talents, gifts, creativity, knowledge, and even your passion aren't enough to break through people's lives.

My experience has been that the further down under God I am, the more powerful and effective my preaching is. It's ironic; the more I make *God* central, the more profoundly he chooses to use *my* preaching to minister his grace. It's also been my experience that the further I am down under God, the more God rattles the gates of hell, bringing about spiritual victories through preaching.

I've discovered at least five paths to getting down under God. These are not in any way formulaic. They're patterns to tune your heart and life into the centrality of God in preaching.

PREACH OUT OF YOUR CORE IDENTITY AS SHEPHERD

Nothing is more critical for pastors today than for them to regain their biblical identity. Wrong identity always leads to wrong preaching. If you consider yourself simply a preacher, your identity isn't complete. Preaching is only one activity of the shepherd. If you only see yourself as a crafter and deliverer of words, you'll lack the motive and force of preaching, which is the shaping, feeding, caring for, and protecting of souls. A shepherd's goal is not simply to impress people with great preaching. Our consuming passion is to care for the people of God.

This is one reason I don't like to be called "preacher." I realize that this is a cultural norm in some parts of the country. But it also communicates a deep misunderstanding about our calling. If all we do is preach (and if that's what our people know us for), there will never be that shepherd-sheep relationship and resulting trust, care, and love that is so crucial to our ministry. That lack causes much of the pastor-congregation conflict that has torn its way into countless churches. If all we are and do is preach, it makes it pretty easy for churches to swap out voices for the latest and greatest. It also makes it easy for preachers to swap congregations when they don't see results from their preaching.

I firmly believe a pastor needs to return to God's ancient identity for a pastor, which is a shepherd. Think about these passages:

- "Shepherd your people with your staff, the flock of your inheritance" (Micah 7:14a).

- "Keep watch over yourselves and all the flock of which the Holy Spirit has made you overseers. Be shepherds of the church of God, which he bought with his own blood" (Acts 20:28).

- "Be shepherds of God's flock that is under your care, serving as overseers—not because you must, but because you are willing, as God wants you to be" (1 Peter 5:2a).

Notice that both of the New Testament passages above encourage us to *be* shepherds. Shepherding is all about *being* before *doing*. We do what we do because we are who we are—shepherds.

When the topic of shepherding is discussed, most pastors gravitate toward the *doing*. They'll say, "Shepherding is pastoral counseling." "Shepherding is visiting." "Shepherding is personally signing the letters you write." "Shepherding is having a meet-and-greet time after the service." "Shepherding is saying, 'Our church is people.'" Not only are such descriptions woefully inadequate in capturing the essence of shepherding, they don't even begin to address what's really at the heart of shepherding, which is pastoral identity. The freedom and joy of ministry comes when you escape the task list and begin living out who you are.

> The freedom and joy of ministry comes when you escape the task list and begin living out who you are.

Shepherd-leadership is an all-encompassing metaphor. Shepherds have a stewardship responsibility for their flocks. This means that as they minister, at times they need to be servants. At times they need to be strong leaders. They may need to rescue their sheep. They need to discipline their sheep. They need to defend their sheep. They may find it necessary to shepherd with a staff. Or they may find it necessary to shepherd with a rod. However, all of these actions flow from the meta-identity of shepherd.

Identifying their leadership style has led many pastors away from true pastoral identity. Pastors define their identity based on specific actions (servant-leader, visionary, manager). The ancient metaphor of shepherd, however, embodies almost all leadership styles and the variety of spiritual gifts and natural talents. It says, "As a shepherd, I will assess what my flock needs at any moment and will ensure its health, safety, and vitality."

A flock cannot thrive with only servant leadership. It cannot grow with only visionary leadership. Any one leadership style is insufficient to care for a flock. A flock requires a shepherd who's willing to do all that is necessary to help the flock flourish (which does not mean the flock will always be happy). But a pastor never needs to leave his or her core identity and calling as a shepherd to meet the needs of the flock.

> ultimately the shepherd realizes that he or she is down under the chief shepherd.

Preaching is one of the ways, a primary way, a pastor shepherds the flock. Ultimately the shepherd realizes that he or she is down under the Chief Shepherd. Jesus Christ is shepherding his flock through a pastor's life and preaching. Far more is going on during the sermon time than just Christian communication. Jesus Christ is personally reaching out to his people and leading them into the safe pastures of his grace. What an incredible experience!

GETTING DOWN

Want to set the pace for being seen as a shepherd? Try one of these:

- *Preach a message on what it means to be a shepherd.*

- *Preach a message expressing your reasons for preaching.* Communicate the fact that you preach in order to love, nurture, care for, and protect the flock.

- *Give plenty of time for response and "soul care" in your preaching services.* If we're shepherds—not just preachers—that means the effect of our preaching is more important that the preaching itself.

Getting down under God is ultimately a transfer of trust. We get down under God when we stop trusting ourselves for effectiveness in preaching and start trusting God. Yet many pastors, wanting to increase their effectiveness, resort to improving the mechanics of preaching. The thought is if I do a better job executing the task of preaching, then I'll be a more effective preacher. Although we should constantly strive toward sharpening the edge of our preaching skills—to speak on behalf of almighty God demands the pursuit of excellence—we ought never to do so at the expense of dependence upon God.

I remember when this hit home early in my ministry. The phone rang. "Pastor Glenn, can you come to the hospital? We were in a serious accident and really need you." "No problem, I'll be there," I said with confidence.

But there was a problem; as I raced to the hospital I couldn't think of anything to say to the family members. I thought, "I have a degree in theology, I should be able to come up with something!" I came up empty and started to panic, so I cried out to God for wisdom and direction. "God, if you don't help me, I have nothing to give!"

I tried to provide comfort, encouragement, practical guidance, and wise counsel as one of the family members passed away; but I felt so inadequate. At the end of the day, I couldn't remember much of what I had said and wondered if I had actually helped anyone!

Weeks after the funeral, however, the family members and friends thanked me for my effective ministry to them. I was truly stunned. What God used most in that chaotic time wasn't my competence but my simple dependence upon him. Reliance on the Lord overrode my skill and training.

> we get down under god when we stop trusting ourselves for effectiveness in preaching and start trusting god.

Here's what I learned: The more we do something and the better we get at it, the more tempted we are to depend on our own skills and competencies rather than to rely on God. We shouldn't try to replace dependency with competency. I'm not saying that you shouldn't increase your skills as a pastor. I'm saying that even if you have a Ph.D., it can't replace a Sc.D. (simple childlike dependence). As the Bible says in Proverbs 3:5-6:

"Trust in the Lord with all your heart, and lean not on your own understanding; in all your ways acknowledge Him, and He shall direct your paths" (New King James Version).

A practical habit I developed years ago, at the suggestion of a pastoral mentor, was to pray through every line of my sermon before I preached it. Notice I didn't say *rehearse* every line (you may need to do that too); I said *pray* through every line. I've done this for as long as I can remember, and I consider it one of the most important components of my preparation process. What I pray for is God's pleasure and will in each thought that I've developed in my study process. I take each thought and even each sentence (especially the ones I think are pretty good), and say, "Lord, is this what you want to say to the congregation? Will it please you if I say this? And if I say this, will you bless it with your power? If this is not what you want me to say, then I'll change it right here." This doesn't take the place of prayer prior to and during the preparation and study process, but rather is a time once again to surrender to God's direction and pleasure.

> A practical habit I developed years ago, at the suggestion of a pastoral mentor, was to pray through every line of my sermon before I preached it.

This habit has been a constant reminder that I'm completely dependent on God in my preaching. It helps dissuade me from thinking that I can carry a service on my own, through my natural abilities to deliver a sermon. It forces me to remember that even after applying the best preparation methods, if my preaching has any effect it will be only because God was pleased to speak through it.

Another thing I often do before I preach is kneel in prayer to posture my inner attitude. Posturing the body in such a humble manner has a way of ordering our inner attitude. It's nothing more—but also nothing less—than showing God and others how we're feeling inside.

We need to go beyond just saying that we're dependent on God in our preaching; we need to incorporate habits and actions that demonstrate it. Of course, beware of the possibility of empty habits. The most important thing is to cultivate a heart that's fully dependent on God in preaching and in all of life.

GETTING DOWN

To model dependence upon God, try these simple things:

• ***Begin dividing your sermon preparation time equally between study and prayer.*** Prayer is a tangible habit of dependence.

• ***Begin practicing the habit of kneeling or lying prostrate in private before your preaching moment.*** Notice the change in attitude that it produces.

• ***Watch out for "tricks" that you may be relying on in the pulpit to elicit a response.*** Catch phrases, humor, stories, intonation, and flamboyance can all be devices that we rely on instead of on God. They're not bad in themselves; just be sure you're not trusting in them as the strength of your preaching.

PRAY FOR GOD'S "SACRED ANOINTING"

We need to take our prayers one step further. If you read the ancients, as well as many of God's choice preaching instruments even in our own day, you'll quickly understand that they longed to experience the presence of Jesus in their ministry. This longing is more than just a penchant for the mystical. It was and is a clear understanding that preaching is essentially an encounter with the living Lord Jesus. And although Jesus is present everywhere and at all times, sometimes he chooses to manifest his presence in an extraordinary way. Preaching and the Lord's Supper are two of those places where Jesus has committed his extraordinary presence.

> As the spirit of god blew through the lives of people, there was an incredible bearing of fruit, growth, and blessing.

Many of the church fathers and mystics experienced this special presence. So did men like Robert Murray M'Cheyne (and many other Scottish divines), Evan Roberts, A.W. Tozer, D. Martyn Lloyd-Jones, Jonathan Edwards, Richard Baxter, Martin Bucer, George Whitefield, John Wesley, C.H. Spurgeon, and D.L. Moody. These men testify of encountering Jesus through preaching in such a way that hearts were melted, spiritual victories were gained, repentance and salvation were given, and a prevailing sense of love and affection for Jesus himself was experienced. Often this encounter with the presence of Jesus would happen during the preaching and sometimes just before or after it. In the ministry of Evan Roberts (who ministered during the Welsh revival), the presence would descend on the congregation during the singing of a particular young woman. The Spirit would break the hearts of the congregation even before Roberts preached.[2]

> If we're going to experience lasting transformation through preaching, it will be the result of the spirit's anointing of both pastor and congregation.

What these servants sought and often experienced was, technically speaking, the present ministry of the Holy Spirit. The New Testament, and the book of Acts in particular, is the record of the Spirit's formation of and influence on the early church. As the Spirit of God blew through the lives of people, there was an incredible bearing of fruit, growth, and blessing. Ministry and transformation happened as the Spirit chose to intersect with the lives of people in real time. It's no different today, nor will it ever be. If we're going to experience lasting transformation through preaching, it will be the result of the Spirit's anointing of both pastor and congregation.

Throughout the history of the church, people have given testimony to the present and special ministry of the Holy Spirit. They've been from a variety of theological backgrounds and perspectives. While some have abused it and others through fear have avoided it, many give testimony to what it means to preach with the blessing and anointing of God. This is not a charismatic, pentecostal, reformed, dispensational, or "fill-in-the-blank" issue. Call it what you want, but may we never preach merely from intellect, skill, and flesh.

The anointing of the Spirit in your preaching is everything. It's what grants the freedom, power, authority, and connection with your congregation that transcends your normal abilities. It's what takes the earthen offering you make and transforms it into a spiritual vessel. It's what makes preaching more than oratory. It's what makes communication an encounter with the divine. It's what reaps spiritual fruit. It's what brings about God's purpose and kingdom on earth.

One way I demonstrate my longing and desire for the Spirit's anointing is through a group of men in our church called the "Pastor's Prayer Partners." Before I preach, these men gather around me, lay their hands on me as a sign of blessing and faith, and pray for the Spirit to fill and use me. Then when I leave to preach, they remain in the room and pray for me the entire service. Without a doubt, this is a power source in my preaching life. I sense their prayers and can often tangibly feel God's answer to their prayers on my behalf.

Congregations also experience the anointing of the Spirit. The Spirit must energize and open people's hearts if they're to receive the blessing of the preached Word. The congregation is as needy of the Spirit's touch as the pastor. Without the Spirit, our congregation is just an audience rather than a flock of hungry souls. Encourage your congregations to pray and prepare for their encounter with Jesus on Sunday morning. We need to move our congregations beyond just showing up for church and lead them into the attitude of preparing for and expecting to experience the presence of Christ.

The thing that both pastors and congregations have in common is that we must seek the Spirit's ministry among us. God desires to be sought and pursued. Think of these Bible passages that direct us to seek God:

> "But from there you will seek the Lord your God, and you will find Him if you seek Him with all your heart and with all your soul" (Deuteronomy 4:29, NKJV).

> "But without faith it is impossible to please Him, for he who comes to God must believe that He is, and that He is a rewarder of those who diligently seek Him" (Hebrews 11:6, NKJV).

This seeking of God, this longing after him, is primarily something we do in the context of prayer. We must constantly pray for the Spirit's touch upon our preaching. I never assume that the Spirit will touch my lips and anoint my preaching. And although I know that I cannot earn or deserve the Spirit's energizing, I can long for it, and by doing so I bring pleasure to him and open my life to his present power.

> The spirit must energize and open people's hearts if they're to receive the blessing of the preached word.

GETTING DOWN

How about making the present ministry of the Holy Spirit an important part of your worship service? You could:

- *Have a pre-service prayer time, encouraging people to seek the Spirit's touch.*

- *Revive the practice of having a prayer of invocation.* Invite the special presence of God to fall on your gathering.

- *Develop a "Pastor's Prayer Partners" ministry.*

SEEK TO BE FILLED WITH GOD

We've used the educational model in pastoral ministry far too long. Ministry is so much more than being filled with knowledge and then transferring that knowledge to others. There's nothing wrong with knowledge; I value it enough to have earned two doctorates. Effective pastors need to be careful and accurate theologians. With that said, knowledge *about* God does not fill us; but the knowledge *of* God can fill us. And only when God himself has filled our hearts and lives do we have the capacity to preach with endurance and long-term effectiveness.

Richard Baxter said it this way: "The preacher that speaks as if he saw the face of God affects my heart more, though with common words, than one with the most exquisite preparations."[3]

To have a heart that sees "the face of God," Baxter suggested: "See that the work of saving grace be thoroughly wrought in your own souls. Take heed to yourselves, lest you be void of that saving grace of God which you offer to others, and be strangers to the effectual working of that gospel which you preach."[4]

I'm not advocating that pastors abandon intense preparation and diligent study; in fact, I would call you to more faithful, intense study. What I am saying is that if all we're doing is studying, preparing, exegeting, parsing, outlining, illustrating, and delivering, we're missing the mark completely. A significant amount of our time and energy as pastors needs to be spent in pursuing a relationship with God. And the result of this relationship will be personal growth in maturity and Christlikeness.

Are you living and experiencing the things that you're preaching? Are you modeling the character of one in pursuit of God in how you spend your time? Is your preparation time altogether cerebral? Are you deliberately stoking the fires of devotion to God in your life? How are you wanting people to define you—as a smart pastor or a Christlike pastor (the two don't need to be antithetical)? These are the kinds of questions that get at the heart of living a God-filled life. And we need to ask them.

> A significant amount of our time and energy as pastors needs to be spent in pursuing a relationship with God.

Many of us were taught that a capacity to preach is earned in the study. But I've found that study without a heart for God results in dryness and fatigue. Sustained effectiveness in preaching comes through the process of making relationship with God primary. As I daily place my personal life down under God through devotion, worship, confession, and obedience, my capacity to preach increases. As I balance study and devotion, my life is more prepared to preach over the long haul.

At the heart of most pastoral burnout is an overemphasis on doing over being. When you try doing what you're not personally living (being) you will crash. We can preach on healthy marriage without having one. We can preach on worship without doing it. We can preach on heaven and not long for it. We can preach on hell and not be in terror. We can preach on the love of God and not know what it is to experience it. Nothing can be more devastating to a pastor than doing without being.

Gregory of Nazianzus said: "A man must himself be cleansed before cleansing others. Become wise so that he may make others wise. Become light and then give light. Draw near to God and so bring others near. Be hallowed then hallow them. Be possessed of hands to lead others by the hand of wisdom."[5]

The solution is to value being over doing. In practical terms you may need to slow down or reduce the quantity of truth you're preaching and focus on quality by embodying smaller portions of truth. For example, rather than preaching a series of unrelated messages, choose a theme that you can focus on for a given period of time. Encourage the congregation, yourself included, to not only assimilate the information related to that theme but to find practical ways to embody it as well. Again, make yourself a part of that process. As you do this, you'll not only have the opportunity to personally live what you're preaching, but you'll model for your congregation the right way to assimilate truth.

The bottom line: Don't settle for an empty soul in ministry. Don't replace God with the duties of preaching. A heart for God is the only way to experience sustained strength and passion in the pulpit. Don't neglect it.

GETTING DOWN

Want to cultivate a heart for God? Try these things:

• ***Practice a weekly or monthly "Day Sabbatical."*** Get away with your Bible and a journal. Spend the day in the Bible and in prayer. Record your thoughts and your feelings in your journal.

• ***Practice "Personal Worship."*** Because pastors are usually leading the worship service, they often don't have the opportunity of fully engaging in worship. Get the videotapes of a neighboring church, and make a habit of listening to them during the week and worshipping along. Be sure you watch somebody else's service so that you're not always critiquing your own. A fresh perspective helps to revive your own ministry.

• ***Instead of attending the next programming conference, attend a spiritual retreat instead.*** Better yet, hold one of your own. Retreat to a place alone for a weekend simply to focus on your relationship with God. This is like pouring cool water on parched lips. As you're filled with God personally, you'll develop the capacity to minister for him publicly. By the way, spiritual retreats should be required of pastors by their congregations and leaders.

In the movie *Chariots of Fire,* runner Eric Liddell said that the reason he wanted to run was because he felt God's pleasure when he ran. I wonder how many pastors preaching today would say the same about their work. Do we sense God's pleasure when we preach? We should and we can.

I know the love-hate relationship pastors often have with preaching. It's grueling and rewarding at the same time. It's a major stress and a major relief. It's pleasure and it's torture. But we must realize that preaching pleases God.

Listen to the words of the Apostle Paul: "For since in the wisdom of God the world through its wisdom did not know him, God was *pleased* through the foolishness of what was preached to save those who believe" (1 Corinthians 1:21, italics added).

> Do we sense god's pleasure when we preach? we should and we can.

The magnificent thing about God's pleasure in preaching is that we can tap into and sense his pleasure. And God's pleasure creates pleasure in us. Nothing in life is greater than knowing we are involved in something that pleases the Lord.

Preaching down under God, therefore, involves making God our ultimate audience. We get trapped into thinking that people are our primary audience when really they're secondary. Preaching is a part of the entire worship offering that we make to God and therefore involves God directly.

We sometimes mess this up when we fall into the relevance trap. When we preach to ultimately please or attract people rather than God, we lose sight of our primary audience. Why do we become fearful in the pulpit? Because we preach to people rather than for God's pleasure. Why do we compromise our message? Because we're trying to tickle people's ears rather than please God. Why don't we always sense joy in preaching? Because we're focusing on the human elements of preaching rather than the divine pleasure of God.

So how do we know that we have pleased God in our preaching? Let me give you five ways.

* ***When we know we have preached something difficult in the face of fear.*** Jesus often stepped over fear of the Pharisees and hostile Jews to preach the kingdom of God. We please God in preaching when we don't succumb to fear, and we preach what God asks us to preach, regardless of the consequences. Think of where the church would be if Jesus, the apostles, or the prophets would have allowed fear to dictate their preaching plans.

- **When God speaks to people in a personal way.** Jesus spoke to Zacchaeus, the Samaritan woman, Nicodemus, and others in a personal manner. God is pleased when our preaching reaches the individual, not just the masses.

- **When we preach with joy in God.** In the parable of the lost sheep, the reaction of the one who finds the lost sheep is telling. It says, "And when he finds it, he *joyfully* puts it on his shoulders and goes home. Then he calls his friends and neighbors together and says, '*Rejoice* with me; I have found my lost sheep.' I tell you that in the same way there will be more *rejoicing* in heaven over one sinner who repents than over ninety-nine righteous persons who do not need to repent" (Luke 15:5-7, italics added). When God works through our preaching to rescue a soul, bind up the wounded, or bring someone to repentance, we can please God by responding with joy. After all, *he* does!

- **When spiritual victories are won.** Jesus' preaching freed people from the guilt and bondage of sin. We please God in our preaching when we aim at ushering people into spiritual freedom, forgiveness, restoration, and redemption.

> Jesus' victory over Satan is an under-discussed aspect of Jesus' life and ministry.

- **When the tactics of Satan are exposed and diminished.** Jesus' victory over Satan is an under-discussed aspect of Jesus' life and ministry. Jesus defeated Satan at every turn, exposed him for the fraud he is, and ultimately destroyed his power in the resurrection. We can please God in our preaching when we expose Satan and his tactics and regularly remind the church that Satan is a defeated foe.

Who are you preaching for? Whose evaluation are you seeking? Make God your audience, and you'll be one step closer to preaching down under.

Preaching down under is about preaching with a clear sight of God's authority and sovereignty over us. I commend to you this view and practice of preaching as the only way that exalts God into his proper place. So long as we try to keep God at bay in our preaching, and so long as we exalt ourselves over him, stealing his glory every chance we get, we settle for the meager existence of words-peddlers, or worse, charlatans. But as we settle in under the umbrella of God's greatness and glory, doing all we can to magnify the worthiness of God in our preaching ministry, we emerge as vessels through whom God may choose to work mightily without the risk of stealing the glory that belongs to him and him alone.

See you down under.

GETTING DOWN

How are you cultivating your joy in God as you preach? I suggest that you schedule a post-preaching review. Think about what God seemed to accomplish through your latest message. Then join God in his rejoicing. Spend time thanking God and delighting in the fruit of your preaching.

GO DEEPER

If you want to pursue the theme of "Preaching Down Under" further, I recommend you read the following books:

The Supremacy of God in Preaching, by John Piper

The Reformed Pastor, by Richard Baxter

Brothers, We Are Not Professionals, by John Piper

Reforming Pastoral Ministry, by John Armstrong (Ed.)

NOTES

1. Martyn Lloyd-Jones, *Revival* (Westchester, IL: Crossway Books, 1987), 295.

2. Visit www.revival-library.org for details on the Welsh revival and many other revival movements.

3. Richard Baxter, *The Reformed Pastor* (Edinburgh: Banner of Truth Trust, 1974), 119. Adapted by John Fanella. Used by permission.

4. Richard Baxter, *The Reformed Pastor,* 53.

5. Gregory Nazianzus, Oration, 2.71, *Nicene and Post-Nicene Fathers,* Second Series, Vol. 7, modernized by John Fanella. Used by permission.

E. Glenn Wagner is senior pastor of Calvary Church in Charlotte, North Carolina. He is the author of several books including *Escape From Church, Inc.* and *The Church You've Always Wanted.* He is also a columnist for Rev. Magazine. You can e-mail him at egw@calvarychurch.com.

chapter twelve

PREACHING:
HOW TO START
AND STOP

BY STUART BRISCOE

INTRIGUING INTRODUCTIONS

At the risk of getting things back to front, I usually develop my introduction to the sermon after the rest is complete. I admit there was a time when I would simply stand up and say, "would you open your Bibles, please?" while that is perfectly valid, it's not exactly attention grabbing for a lot of people—particularly if they haven't brought a Bible or if they can see one in the pew in front of them but are afraid to pick it up because they have no idea where to find the first Epistle of peter and are not about to demonstrate the fact by fumbling. so a little thought about introductions can go a long way. The opening paragraph of my outline would not always be the introduction to the sermon because introductions are often most effective if they have an element of surprise.

The Keswick Convention in the north of England is an annual event. When I was young, it was the British Super Bowl of evangelicalism. My family attended every year just on Wednesday because my dad had a store and that meant only a half-day closing. It was a bore. I used to sit there on a hard bench in the big tent on a warm summer afternoon, thinking of lots of places I'd rather be. On Wednesdays the subject was always the lordship of Christ. In those days I approached that subject with a considerable degree of trepidation, so you can imagine my annual frame of mind as convention time rolled around, and once more I deposited my unwilling youthfulness on an unyielding bench knowing full well I would be exposed to unpalatable truth.

> I deposited my unwilling youthfulness on an unyielding bench knowing full well I would be exposed to unpalatable truth.

On one occasion I was sitting there wondering how long an hour was going to last and paying such scant attention to the proceedings that I was unaware the meeting had begun, when suddenly a big voice bellowed, "The way to up is down!" There was a sort of fluttering among the people as when doves in a shed suspect a cat might be in the vicinity. I looked up, and there was a tall man with wavy gray hair—at least that's how he looked to me as a kid all those years ago. He just stood there looking out at the people quite sternly. There was a very long, dramatic pause. I became quite nervous. Then he bellowed, "The way to down is up!"

That introduction was unforgettable, as is evidenced by the fact that I still remember it. Here I sit more than fifty years later remembering as if it were yesterday the opening lines of a sermon I didn't want to hear. I found out subsequently that the preacher's name was Donald Grey Barnhouse. But more importantly, I discovered the principle he taught that day. He gave an exposition of what had been stated less dramatically by Peter: " 'God opposes the proud but gives grace to the humble.' Humble yourselves, therefore, under God's mighty hand, that he may lift you up in due time" (1 Peter 5:5-6).

To my mind this was a classic introduction because it not only grabbed my attention but was succinct and sharply focused. It encapsulated an entire message in memorable form and placed a rather abstract, anachronistic expression in arresting, modern terms. Now we are not all called "Barnhouse," but we can all work on our introductions.

It's humbling for preachers to bear in mind how little people remember of what they say, and even more disconcerting when you realize the things people find memorable. They remember your mistakes—if your teeth fly out, they will never forget that. But the good news is they like and tend to remember good stories. So preachers should think of stories that will not only aid memory but will also serve as attention-grabbing introductions and form entrances to the structure of their sermons.

I started a series of talks on motivation one day with this story:

Jill and I arrived in Kimberley in South Africa and were met at the airport by a little lady whom we had not previously met. Fortunately, she recognized us, and, as we were getting our bags, she surprised me by saying, "Would you like to see the hole?"

And so, being British, I said, "I beg your pardon?" If I'd been American I would have said, "Huh?" I had no idea what she was talking about, but being terribly British and excruciatingly polite I said, "We would love to see the hole. Thank you very much indeed."

She said, "Would you like to see where you're staying first, or would you like to go to the hole immediately?"

Recognizing that her enthusiasm knew no bounds, I said, "Immediately, let's go right away."

> preachers should think of stories that will not only aid memory but will also serve as attention-grabbing introductions.

(In parentheses, let me point out that this strange occurrence does tend to get people's attention. They're thinking, "What hole? Why is this strange lady so excited about a hole? What in the world is going on?")

As we were driving along she said, "It's the biggest man-made hole in the world, you know."

I replied quite truthfully, "No. I didn't know that."

"Oh, yes," she replied with great enthusiasm, "and it was dug with very primitive implements."

"Like what?" I inquired.

"Oh," she said, "little hand shovels and leather buckets and a system of pulleys. And it's a mile in circumference and hundreds of feet deep."

She went on, hardly stopping to take a breath. "It was awful. There was rioting and famine and plague and murder. It was awful. But people traveled from all over the world to participate in digging this hole!"

It was obvious to me by this time that the little lady assumed that I knew all about the hole of her dreams, and I was intent on hiding my ignorance as long as possible. But by this time, I was getting really interested.

She said, "It used to be a hill, you know."

Now that really got me. "Used to be a hill?"

She said, "Yes, indeed. It used to be a hill."

By this time we'd arrived, and sure enough, there was no hill, just a hole. One mile in circumference. Hundreds of feet deep. My curiosity was totally stimulated by this time, so I asked, "Why would people come from all over the world to start digging on top of a hill to make the biggest hole in the world in the middle of nowhere?"

She was eager to explain. "Well, it's very simple really. Some little boys were playing on the hill one day, throwing pebbles to each other. An old gentleman walking past saw the sun glint on one of the pebbles and he caught it, examined it, and immediately recognized it. A diamond. The Kimberly Diamond Mine was born!"

And that's how you turn a hill into the biggest hole in the world. Diamonds lying around do tend to motivate.

I've told the story many times, and people are usually interested and intrigued by it. Of course, we're not called to be intriguing raconteurs, so we have to make a point from the story. In this case I wanted to point out that when adequately motivated, for good or evil, human beings are capable of remarkable feats, but when insufficiently motivated they will almost always live far below potential.

> when adequately motivated, for good or evil, human beings are capable of remarkable feats.

It's hard to imagine circumstances under which people could have been persuaded to leave home and kindred, travel to the African veld, endure incredible hardship and danger simply to dig a hole. But greed being what it is and the desire to get rich quick being a powerful motivational factor, they went, proving to me without doubt that one of the most important factors in life is motivation. The series then developed the theme of motivation from a study of Paul's autobiographical passages, which allow a look into the head of the great apostle to see what motivated him, what made him tick.

WAVELENGTHS   John Stott quips that many people regard preachers as "six days invisible and one day incomprehensible."

My guess is that the two are linked. Some preachers literally stay sequestered in their studies so that they have little contact with people where they live. Others do it metaphorically in that they spend all their time wading through the murky depths of theology and philosophy without ever setting foot in the mundane shallows where most people live their lives. Both sets of preachers will have difficulty understanding how people think, which means their listeners will have difficulty understanding what these preachers say. Invisible can mean incomprehensible.

> John stott quips that many people regard preachers as "six days invisible and one day incomprehensible."

Craig Skinner stated bluntly, "Any speaker who assumes that his audience thinks and feels exactly as he does will always be wrong." Preachers must keep in touch with the world of their people, not at the expense of study but always with relevance in mind. This is particularly important when introductions are being crafted. The introduction not only serves to introduce a topic of interest to the people, thereby arresting their attention, but it also serves to introduce the preacher in a way that will intrigue the listener. This guy understands where I'm living. I'm glad to know this preacher isn't living on cloud nine while I'm struggling in pit twelve. Oh, he knows about that movie I saw and didn't understand. Ah, he's got an opinion on what the president said this week. I wonder what he thinks. All these reactions and many more can and should be buzzing in the congregation's minds after an appropriate beginning.

For example, during the 1992 presidential election, Vice President Dan Quayle made a critical comment about Murphy Brown having a baby out of wedlock. The fact that Murphy Brown was a fictional TV character didn't inhibit the eruption of a furious debate on the subject of family values. All that was necessary to get people's attention the next week, and in fact to embark on an eight-week series on values, was my opening comment, "Murphy and Dan have been having problems this week." The congregation laughed, some a little nervously, and we were under way to pointing out the irony of the situation and the significance of the subject. This led, of course, to a statement about the necessity of values, an explanation of what we mean by values, an exploration of the way we arrive at values, and an evaluation of the values that significantly determine our lifestyles.

Next week I will preach on relationships, from John 15. I'm particularly concerned about the fact that in the church whenever we talk about relationships, we almost always deal with marital situations, despite the fact that up to a third of the adult population, and therefore a third of many congregations, are single. So I intend to read from a questionnaire sent out by a personal introduction service. This will certainly get the attention of the singles, but it will also be interesting to married folks who have little idea of the particular stresses and strains of single life in the modern world. For example, here are some of the questions raised in the questionnaire:

- 1. Are you in a dead-end relationship or in a relationship of convenience?

- 2. Are you tired of meeting people who in the beginning say they're everything you want and then you find out within six months that they're totally different people?

- 3. Are you tired of having your intelligence insulted by the games you have to play to meet someone special?

- 4. Are you tired of meeting men or women whom you fall in love with and then discover that you're not the only one in their lives?

- 5. Do you feel unsafe with the conventional methods of meeting people?

It will not be difficult to move from this sampling of issues that confront people in their search for authentic relationships to a discussion of the factors that make for the deep relationships for which the human heart craves. People are always interested in relationships.

It's time I came to a conclusion on the subject of introductions. My son Pete was invited to preach in his seminary chapel shortly before graduation, an honor afforded to only two students each year. So his proud parents went to listen, while looking appropriately humble. After a rather tepid introduction from one of the professors, Pete strode to the microphone, all six feet, five inches of him, and without hesitation said, "You never get a second chance to make a first impression." It wasn't original, but it was powerful, and it's true of introductions. You don't get a second chance to make a first impression, so take the one chance you get and make it work.

> people are always interested in relationships.

WELL-CRAFTED CONCLUSIONS

A number of years ago I was invited to speak at Peninsula Bible Church in Palo Alto, California. The senior pastor, Ray Stedman, who was a dear friend, introduced me with typical humor. "Friends," he said, "Stuart's here again. I guess I should say something about him, but I don't know what to say." He paused and then went on, with a twinkle in his eye, "Oh, yes! There is one thing you probably don't know about Stuart Briscoe. He's the man of whom Billy Graham once said, 'Who?' " The audience laughed and I spoke.

Some time later Ray was a guest in our home, and as I introduced him to my younger son, Pete, who was probably thirteen at the time, I related the above story. To my surprise, Pete did not laugh, even though he has a great sense of humor. He turned to Ray and said, "Dr. Stedman, you think you know my father, but it's obvious you don't. Because anyone who knows my father knows that he needs no introduction, but he sure needs a conclusion!"

> "anyone who knows my father knows that he needs no introduction, but he sure needs a conclusion!"

My reputation for needing a conclusion goes back to the first sermon I ever preached. I was seventeen at the time and had been given the subject "The Church at Ephesus." I'd worked hard at learning as much as I could about a church which, up until that time, I had not known existed. When the great day for my maiden sermon arrived, I buried my head in my notes, took off, and did not look up until I had finished my first point. Looking at the clock, which I feared would barely have moved, I was dumbstruck to find that I'd already exceeded my time and still had two more points to go! I blurted out in embarrassment, "I'm terribly sorry. I don't know how to stop." Whereupon an old gentleman sitting in the back row shouted, "Just shut up and sit down!" That's one way of arriving at a conclusion without arriving at a conclusion.

KNOWING WHEN TO END

Some sermons are like golf balls, which have a tendency to roll on after they've stopped. Perhaps preachers who suffer from that tendency take comfort from the fact that Paul in his letter to the Philippians wrote "finally" well before he finished! He could have said "lastly" and then lasted! The apostle's example notwithstanding, it's good for a sermon to arrive at a conclusion in timely fashion. A sermon that has difficulty stopping can quickly undo any good it achieved while it was moving along.

A preacher who goes on after he has finished will quickly irritate his hearers if they suspect that he doesn't know how to wind it all up because he hasn't prepared himself for the final moment. They'll quickly resent being required to be spectators of his work in progress while the line at the restaurant gets ever longer. But far more importantly, the congregation should depart from hearing the sermon with minds and hearts full of information rather than irritation. The way the preacher concludes the sermon will have much to do with the way the people leave and what they carry away with them. The conclusion of a sermon should have similarities to the way in which items purchased at a supermarket are packaged and delivered to the car. In both cases everything is neatly accounted for, put in place, and presented in manageable form ready to be taken home.

> The congregation should depart from hearing the sermon with minds and hearts full of information rather than irritation.

CRAFTING THE CONCLUSION

A sermon that has been effective will have addressed the whole person. Mind, will, and emotions will have felt the impact of the preaching of the Word. The conclusion should briefly, and I emphasize briefly, summarize the salient points, which hopefully have made an impact on the mind during the course of the preaching. The emotional and motivational force of the information that has been intellectually appropriated should be underlined, if possible, by an illustration, and the challenge to obedience or dependence that the preaching will have prompted should be made abundantly clear. It should be apparent that preaching that incorporates all three dimensions is likely, under the Spirit's operation, to produce response.

It should also be clear that preachers must studiously avoid manipulating a response that may subsequently abort. Undue challenges without adequate explanations are a case in point. Wills pushed to respond to truth that minds have not grasped and assimilated rarely produce fruits of righteousness. Emotions played upon by polished motivators before the Spirit has had time to take the truth home to the heart will dive as promptly to disillusionment as they leaped to response. At the same time, preaching that lays out truth in a flat, unemotional, unchallenging manner can hardly be mistaken for the truth of the Bible, which gladdens the heart, feeds the mind, challenges the will, and changes lives. All this to show that the conclusion is more important than we may have been led to believe.

I believe that sermons should usually end with prayer. When I lead the congregation in prayer at the end of a sermon, I generally introduce it by saying something like, "We're now going to pray, and it may be that you wish to respond to the message in your own heart to the Lord. But you may not be sure how to phrase what you want to say or how to express what you're feeling. My prayer could be your prayer. If you find that it matches what is going on in your heart at this time, make it your own. You don't need to say it out loud. God is not hard of hearing." The prayer then is a simple summary of the things that one could reasonably expect people would want to say to the Lord. I find these few moments at the end of a sermon are usually deeply significant. A stillness settles over the congregation as men and women talk to the Lord after they've given careful attention to what he had to say to them.

> A stillness settles over the congregation as men and women talk to the Lord after they've given careful attention to what he had to say to them.

In some traditions a more formalized "invitation" is extended at the end of a service. In a large auditorium or stadium, this gives opportunity for follow-up of those who may respond to an evangelistic message, but would not be reached any other way. In regular church services the situation is different, but the invitation can be helpful. It may give an opportunity for those who wish to make an external demonstration of their response to the Word to do so. The way they do this may take different forms. Raising a hand, standing in place, walking down the aisle, or kneeling at a Communion rail are all common examples. There's no doubt that this type of activity can solidify for some people the action they take in their hearts, and it also can lead people to a confession of their faith. However, it can also become a substitute for the confession with the mouth (or a clearly articulated statement of faith), which Paul shows is a means of other people hearing the Word and coming to faith (see Romans 10:9-14).

In my pastoral preaching I bear in mind that there's a very wide variety of people sitting in the pews and that it's very easy for some of them to be either put off by a certain concluding approach to the sermon or utterly confused by it. Accordingly, we offer a variety of opportunities for people to respond if they wish. We point out that there are pastors standing at the front of the sanctuary if they wish to talk to a pastor. On the other hand, we tell the people that we have a room off the sanctuary called "The Quiet Corner," where those who prefer that approach may go to pray or talk in peaceful surroundings and find help from a layperson. This way we offer something for those who don't mind coming up to the front and something for those who would find it totally intimidating. There's something for those who will only talk to a pastor and something for those who would run a mile rather than talk to a pastor.

Some people don't want to go anywhere, front or back, and they don't want to talk to anybody, pastor or layperson, but they do want help. So for them we have cards in the pews on which they can state whatever it is they want us to know; they can either hand them in at the information center or mail them in when they get home and have had time to think about it a little further. Those who may be interested in more mundane questions, we guide to the information stations. This way we do not pressure people into a response they might not be ready for and that could be counterproductive, but at the same time we do not make it easy for people to disregard the importance of the Word preached and the necessity for them to respond.

> we do not pressure people into a response they might not be ready for and that could be counterproductive.

LEAVE PEOPLE THINKING

Finally, "Points to Ponder" are part of the sermon outline that's distributed to all the members of the congregation. These serve as a provocative concluding summary and response so everybody is confronted with stimulants to thought and action—which is exactly what we hope the preaching will achieve.

This chapter is from an upcoming Group Publishing book titled *Preacher It!* which is due to release in December of 2003. Stuart Briscoe was born in Millom, Cumbria, England, in 1930. After beginning a banking career and preaching ministry in England, in 1970 he became senior pastor of Elmbrook Church, near Milwaukee, Wisconsin, where he served for thirty-three years, helping to build Elmbrook into the leading church it is today. Brisco has authored dozens of books and is in demand around the world for his preaching and teaching.

chapter thirteen

PREACHING FOR DISCIPLESHIP

BY MICHAEL W. FOSS

"You're a good preacher," he said. "But you're not a great preacher. If you want to be a great preacher, call me. I can help." With that, he walked away.

I had seen him waiting in the foyer after worship. When the rest of the worshippers had left, he had approached me. I didn't know him. And when he walked away, I didn't know whether to be angry or flattered. The next day I called a friend who knew the family. I discovered that he had worked in a national church body, had graduate degrees in speech and drama, and had taught those courses as well as debate. I called him that day.

We met at a coffee shop, got acquainted, and then— as abruptly as he had spoken the previous Sunday—he simply said, "When you preach, what do you want to have happen?" "What do you mean?" I asked. "Well, I assume that when you preach you want the hearers to experience something and, perhaps, do something with it."

Most preachers assume that preaching is an end in itself. The task of proclaiming the gospel is a sacred work. As such, somewhere between fear of manipulation and fear of failure, most of us don't have specific outcomes in mind when we preach. My new friend, over the next few months, challenged and grew me. He taught me to take the promise of Scripture seriously that the Word of God will never return empty. God's Word does something. The intent of the preacher maximizes his partnership with the Holy Spirit in the Spirit's work—which alone is eternal.

What's the point? For me, preaching is always faith witness.

I remember a fifteenth-century woodcut by Albrecht Dürer of John the Baptist at the cross. Jesus is on the cross, and John is pointing to him in witness that he is the Savior of the world. The interesting thing about the woodcut is that John's pointing finger is exaggerated. It's lengthened to make it clear that he's not the point; Christ is.

> The task of the preacher is not simply to point to Jesus but through the power of the Holy Spirit to make him present.

Preaching is like that. Preaching as faith witness is never about the preacher but about the One proclaimed. And the task of the preacher is not simply to point to Jesus but through the power of the Holy Spirit to make him present. The first thing a preacher must do, then, is get out of the way.

I love to read or listen to other preachers. Most of the time it's an opportunity for me to be spiritually fed. But there have been occasions when I have had the heartfelt pain of no longer listening to preachers because I'm praying that they'll simply get through it! On other occasions I've had the uncomfortable experience of anticipating an "amen" to end the sermons only to have the preachers continue on. The sacred task of proclamation demands the best of us—so that we can get out of the way for those who hear. The "best of us" means both preparation of content and form as well as an understanding of the changing world in which we seek to present Christ.

OUR EXPERIENCE-BASED CULTURE

In our experience-based world, preachers compete with the nightly news, movies, and other entertainment. When people attend worship, they expect not to be entertained but to be engaged in an experience.

The experience provided by many of our churches worked—in a previous decade. Those who faithfully attend probably still find that experience appropriate. But new generations or generations with an openness to the new presentation of experiences in our culture, find those experiences lacking. What once was a more than adequate presentation of Christ, now can seem flat. For decades the role of many preachers was defined in terms of a "talking head." The pastor shared theological insights from the Bible. The assumption was that such insights would be both understood and integrated into the lives of those who heard.

The reinforcement of the application of these ideas was all around. This was during a time when biblical metaphors and images were clearly taught and used in the culture at large. The Ten Commandments, for example, were upheld as a universal standard for good behavior. Christmas carols were sung unapologetically. Political speeches were filled with biblical phrases and images from both testaments. Our society reinforced the power of the language and image of the Bible. The connection between what the worshippers heard and the world in which they lived was natural.

when Jay Leno can interview adults at a shopping mall and get "Keep off the grass" as one of the Ten commandments, we know our world has changed.

Those days are over. We live in a biblically illiterate world. When Jay Leno can interview adults at a shopping mall and get "Keep off the grass" as one of the Ten Commandments, we know our world has changed. Talking heads no longer work. The natural connection between our message and real life is not made by most people. To say it bluntly, our religious jargon has become nonsensical. I don't mean foolish. I mean not making sense to most people.

Talking heads no longer work because our experiential culture seeks an engagement of the whole person. The connection between head and heart is necessary in preaching in the twenty-first century. That's one of the reasons why stories work so well. Stories engage us both intellectually and emotionally.

Because our listeners are looking for the heart-head connection, they expect to see it in the preacher. When preaching was primarily an intellectual exercise, the authenticity of the preacher was not under review in each and every sermon. Now such integrity is a litmus test. If the hearers cannot sense (both see and feel) the integrity of the preacher's faith, then the skepticism of our time kicks in and the listener checks out.

Preaching for discipleship begins, therefore, with the faith journey of the preacher. The invitation to meet Jesus comes from both the experience of the preacher in meeting Christ and the witness of God's Word. This models the connection between Word and world. It also establishes the credentials of the preacher as an authentic person of faith. Because the preacher has experienced the love of God in Jesus Christ, the invitation to the hearer is to come and share in that experience. The point of the preaching then, as my friend taught me, is to *do* something. This is the confidence of our faith: that preaching does something in the life of the hearer.

> if the hearers cannot sense (both see and feel) the integrity of the preacher's faith, then the skepticism of our time kicks in and the listener checks out.

LIVING WITH THE WORD

Preaching for discipleship springs from the expectations of the preacher. I expect that the Holy Spirit will show up when I preach. When the Holy Spirit shows up, the world changes and people are transformed. This is not my work—it's the fulfillment of the promise of God. Tragically, many preachers don't expect anything to happen when they preach. This lack of confidence in the Holy Spirit excuses a lack of preparation. It also excuses the listener from doing anything with the Word. What would an expectation of change mean in the life of the believer?

I expect that people will still be talking about the sermon on the following Thursday. If the content and experience of the presence of Christ hasn't been that significant, then I don't believe I've done my job. But if people are still thinking and discussing the sermon on Thursday, then the tension of connecting the message with their real life is operative. People will struggle to make this connection if the message intrudes upon their business deals or interactions at school or family life.

This is the tension that preaching for discipleship anticipates. Discipleship means following Jesus. Following Jesus isn't done in the safety of the sanctuary only. Following Jesus means taking our faith into real life. That's why, at Prince of Peace, we say, "The bull's-eye of our ministry is to equip you with a faith that will work in your real life." So our preaching is not just centered in the *what* of faith but also in the *how* of faith. The *what* of faith is made up of our beliefs and values. The *how* of faith is the application, the translation of our beliefs and values into behaviors and attitudes that shape our daily lives. This means that preaching for discipleship is both an invitation to growth in understanding as well as a challenge to growth in practicing our faith.

The challenge of practicing our faith can be put to the listener in many ways. Sometimes I'll challenge the congregation by saying, "What about you?" This phrase carries with it the expectation that what has been spoken ought to have a clear connection to the lives of the hearers. With that expectation come some clear applications. For example, if I've been preaching on the parable of the good Samaritan, I may suggest to teens that a clear application of this may be reaching out to the student at school who's always alone or often ridiculed. For adults I might suggest that spending volunteer time at a local homeless shelter or in the distributing of food at a food bank might be the fulfillment of our Lord's command to be a "neighbor." The suggestion of application not only provides a connection of the text to real life but also creates the opportunity for the listener to think creatively in applying the truth of God's Word into their particular circumstances.

Sometimes preaching for discipleship may contain an invitation to do something right then in worship. Not unlike the altar call of some of our traditions, this immediate exercise of faith expects a response and engagement from the listener. On one occasion people each received a stone as they entered worship. Ushers told them that the reason for the stones would be revealed later. Then, having preached on the need to forgive, we invited everyone to "name the stone" by thinking of a person who should be forgiven or a grudge that should end. The worshippers were then invited into a processional of forgiveness to place their stones in large baskets before the altar. The number of adults and children that came forward was astonishing.

> with the invitation to participate, we also provide a "way out."

But what about those who chose not to participate? We need to respect the listeners. With the invitation to participate, we also provide a "way out." I may use words like these: "If you're not ready, for any reason, to participate in this exercise, please know you don't have to. We respect wherever you are in this spiritual journey of faith. So come, or let this pass you by. But if you're willing, please come."

I've come to expect a response. But I also don't want to manipulate people. By simply acknowledging that there will be those who choose not to engage in an activity, people have the freedom to respond as God moves them.

As a preacher, my expectations are the first step in doing my best. Preparation for preaching takes on an entirely different tenor when we expect the Holy Spirit to do something in the lives of others through what we proclaim.

THE SHAPE OF THE SERMON

Dr. Hans Walter Wolff, a great German Old Testament scholar, was preaching on the prophet Hosea. After some remarks, he stopped and said, "Now I want to speak to the preachers here. We must always remember that for Hosea the Word *through* the prophet was first the Word *to* the prophet. And so it must be for the preacher." His point was that preaching effectively means that the preacher has first *heard* the text in his or her own life. This listening is with the inner ear of the soul. Listening to the text begins with asking questions like "What does God want me to hear for my own walk of faith?" or "What challenge do I hear in this text for me?"

Listening to the Spirit means waiting while the text works on us. Sometimes the waiting is short. At other times the waiting may be long. Our waiting may be active or passive. Passive waiting often takes the form of centering prayer in which one aspect of the Scripture becomes the focal point for our prayer and waiting. Active waiting may include working in the original language, reading secondary sources, or even engaging in conversation with others about the text. Preaching for discipleship assumes that the discipleship of the preacher is influenced by the Word before he or she expects that Word to shape and change the lives of any others. This step also ensures the authenticity of the proclaimed word.

When organizing the sermon, I want to be aware of its dramatic progression. Dramatic progression is the structuring of the sermon so the high point, the essential message, is clearly stated and then the sermon should end. I often use a three-part sermon structure. The first part establishes the cultural or experiential basis for this text. This can be contrasting the text with the world in which we live, or it can be a positive comparison. Once this real-life context has been established, I bring the word of the Scripture to light and hold our life experience up against it. The third point of the sermon is the application

> preparation for preaching takes on an entirely different tenor when we expect the Holy Spirit to do something in the lives of others through what we proclaim.

piece. This is how we can live our discipleship in light of the teaching of God's Word. The dramatic progression of the sermon leads to the final point by engaging the hearer in first identifying with the aspects of life and then hearing and understanding how those aspects are influenced by the text itself.

As I shape the sermon, I must constantly ask myself if the sermon is tangible and relevant for the hearers. This is much easier when I can see how it is the real stuff of life for me! At times I've actually written *tangible and relevant* on my sermon outline. In our biblically illiterate society, I can't assume that those who hear the sermon will see the connections on their own. The more concrete (tangible) I can make the sermon's content, the more likely the hearers will be able to integrate the message into their own situations. The more relevant I can show the text to be, the more likely those Thursday conversations will be occurring the following week.

> The more concrete (tangible) I can make the sermon's content, the more likely the hearers will be able to integrate the message into their own situations.

I've not forgotten listening in on a conversation my daughter had with another telecommunications officer. I was with them until they began to shift into their own jargon. Each field of study has its own language. This language serves as a shorthand for the concepts and aspects of that field. Such a language is very helpful for those who know it. But for those outside the field, it can be profoundly confusing.

Preachers need to use less religious jargon than ever before. Even such a simple word as *grace* has lost its meaning to many people in our culture. When we use such terms, it's important that we define them. I'll often speak of God's grace and then attempt to define it as *the unexpected, unearned love of God in Jesus Christ*. Words like *salvation, redemption, justification,* and *sanctification* have no meaning for many outside the church...and many inside as well! I try to rid my final copy of the sermon of as many of those words as possible. I want to invite people into conversation with the Bible—not have them stuck on terms they don't understand. I'm confident that if they interact with God's Word, they'll be brought to a point of decision making about what they ought to do with the truth of the text.

Preaching for discipleship hopes to engage us in living our faith. This means that ministry is assumed to belong to every person of faith. For years I would use personal stories of pastoral care. Then I began to understand that, even when I was preaching that pastoral care belongs to every member or disciple in the congregation, I was modeling through my stories that pastors do it best.

Now when I use personal stories, I share my partnership with other disciples. I may share my own need for forgiveness. I might tell a story in which I missed an opportunity to witness or to provide care. Or I may tell a story of how I had been cared for. When I share personal stories, I want to do so in a manner that makes it clear that I'm not looking for personal sympathy or judgment. The point of the story isn't me. The point of the story is "us."

> when I share personal stories, I want to do so in a manner that makes it clear that I'm not looking for personal sympathy or judgment.

And I never tell a story about my interaction with family members or friends that puts them in a bad light. When I tell stories about others, I always seek their permission—unless the story has been published or told in the public sphere. I will often ask permission and, having received it, still change pronouns or use different names. This protects peoples' privacy—even if they have given me permission to tell their stories. I believe that it's their option to identify themselves to others if they choose. By following these simple rules, people aren't suddenly surprised or embarrassed by hearing personal stories about them they hadn't anticipated. Since I write sermons weeks in advance, I'll often tell people when their stories will be told. *No surprises* is a great rule in telling stories that involve others.

Since I work from an outline, I provide an outline to the listeners. This is a fill-in-the-blanks outline that follows the progression of the sermon itself. What I find thrilling is the number of people who not only fill in the blanks but also take more lengthy notes on the sermon. Often they'll place the outlines in their Bibles at the place of the text. The point of the outline is to equip people to reflect later on the biblical truth presented in the sermon.

PRESENTATION

It was a remarkable experience. I wasn't preaching that day and had stopped for coffee with others in our community room. Just after the next service had begun, I was walking through the parking lot to my office when a minivan drove up and parked. As a wife and mother opened her door to get out, she spoke loudly and sharply to her husband and then began to get the kids out of the back seat. He replied in a similar manner as he helped another child get out of the vehicle. Then they lowered their voices but kept the sharp conversation going as they entered the building to worship.

I wondered how they would make the transition. Obviously, getting the kids ready for church and then getting there had not been a stress-free experience!

Observing that couple taught me the need to build bridges into worship for people. I so often had assumed that, upon entering our worship space, people were automatically ready to come before God. But that parking-lot squabble suggested otherwise. When people enter worship, we need to give them time to become truly present. We can do this by using the opening moments to make announcements. Or we can begin the preaching task by setting the theme for the day. By using an attention-grabbing object, sketch, or life example as the entry into the biblical topic for the day, we can help people make the transition from the parking lot into worship, from their past week into the presence of the living God. We simply need to be more intentional about helping people catch up with us in our worship so that they are better prepared to experience the message.

> By using an attention-grabbing object, sketch, or life example as the entry into the biblical topic for the day, we can help people make the transition from the parking lot into worship.

Children's sermons can provide another opportunity to invite people into the theme for our worship. Children's sermons function at two levels. The first is an age-appropriate lesson that leads to the adult sermon. By speaking to the children, we invite the adults to listen in, and we also model for them faith conversation with children. The second level is perhaps the most significant. On a macro level, children's sermons make it clear that worship is a place for all of God's children, young and old. When adults see that children are authentically welcomed and addressed, their perception of the church is changed. And when a child responds with a humorous statement, as one frequently will, everyone loosens up!

The key to an effective children's sermon is that the presenter needs to be comfortable with children. That person should be flexible, welcoming the moment when the children take over or sidetrack the message. With the assurance that there will be plenty of time to get back on track, the presenter ought to celebrate the spontaneity of the children. The children's sermon can be one more opportunity to prepare the adults for the coming message. One more bridge is built.

PHYSICAL RESOURCES

The preacher has at his disposal a range of physical resources. I've never forgotten a colleague lamenting how easy it was for him to slip into "FM voice" when he preached. When I asked him what he meant, he explained it was a passive, comforting voice that lacked range or emotional content. Most of us have a much broader range of voice than we utilize. Sometimes we're afraid of being overly emotional—a legitimate concern. But when we do not raise the level or pitch of our voices, the hearer can be lulled into FM stupor. Changes in pace, tone, and pitch that are normal in conversation can be great tools for keeping the listener engaged in the sermon. The content of our preaching, no matter how great, cannot carry the attention of others. Remember, we compete with some of the best presenters in the world in our listeners' subconscious.

I take time to practice my sermon again and again. I look for those moments when I should slow down or speed up my presentation. I play with moments of silence—pauses are one of the most intriguing elements that a preacher can incorporate into a sermon. I also watch for one of my greatest temptations: dropping my voice. Even with a marvelous public address system, if I lower my voice too much, even the most attentive listeners might lose what I have to say. Unfortunately, I tend to do this at precisely the most important points!

The use of our bodies can be a distraction or a help to the hearers. If I move too much or gesture without clear intent, I can appear nervous. If I frequently point my finger to make a point, I risk antagonizing those who resist authority. If I can't make eye contact with my hearers, the integrity of the message might be questioned subconsciously. So I want to discipline my body for the sake of the message. I don't want my body

> The children's sermon can be one more opportunity to prepare the adults for the coming message.

language to get in the way of anyone truly hearing the message and meeting the Savior. Once again, the purpose of all of these concerns is that I get out of the way and let God do what only God can do.

These considerations apply to the use of media as well. I remember using a video clip from the movie *Shine,* to demonstrate the point of my sermon. Unfortunately, I failed to consider that the central character in the clip was playing the piano in a bar as a cigarette dangled from his lips. Some people never got past those two elements to see how the clip applied to the Scripture text for the day. Media can enhance the message, but it must be subordinate to the message. We must use caution so that no aspects get in the way. Our use of media ought to be smooth, and its connection to the sermon clear.

TYPES OF
SERMONS

We can use numerous types of sermons, depending upon the outcome we desire and the message itself. Preaching for discipleship recognizes that different themes may suggest different types of preaching. Didactic sermons are intended to teach. Teaching sermons ought to equip disciples with biblical concepts that can be helpful in personal spiritual growth or in our public witness. Didactic sermons are often best for grounding our hearers in biblical doctrine for the assurance of their faith.

Story sermons generally use a story to present a particular biblical truth to the listeners. The problem with a story sermon is that it requires the listeners to have a certain level of spiritual maturity in order to get the point and apply it to their lives. As I have mentioned before, this isn't as easy as it once was. Consequently, I've chosen not to preach on discipleship using this type of sermon.

> I play with moments of silence—pauses are one of the most intriguing elements that a preacher can incorporate into a sermon.

Skits or dialogues can be used to set up the sermon, but they can also *be* the sermon. Because the outcome for my preaching is discipleship, I want it to demonstrate the tensions of living our faith in the real world and how those tensions can be overcome. The critical concern with dramatic presentations is that they not be performances but invitations to experience the presence and truth of God.

Perhaps the best type of sermon is one in a sermon series. One of the more effective series we've done was titled Marks of Discipleship. We covered six practices of faith that form the core of following Jesus. Three are internal and personal: daily prayer, daily Bible reading, and weekly worship. Three are external and social: serving, both in and beyond Prince of Peace; relating to others for spiritual growth; and giving a tithe. We included helps on how to start or grow an individual's or family's practice of each.

Preaching for discipleship requires a clear vision of the outcomes we hope to achieve. These outcomes include personal growth in understanding and experiencing the grace of God, clear application of biblical truths to life, and specific ways to integrate our faith into our daily lives through our relationships and choices. This kind of preaching results in a sharing of witness and increasing participation in and ownership of the ministry itself.

Michael W. Foss is senior pastor of Prince of Peace, a congregation of the Evangelical Lutheran Church in America in Burnsville, Minnesota. He is a frequent speaker in the areas of leadership development and redesigning the church for a new age of mission and ministry. Foss has authored three books: *Power Surge: 6 Marks of Discipleship for a Changing Church* (Fortress Press, July 2000); *A Servant's Manual: Christian Leadership for Tomorrow* (Fortress Press, July 2002); and *What Really Matters: 30 Devotions for Church Leadership Teams* (Group Publishing, June 2003).

chapter fourteen

PREACHING TO THE DE-CHURCHED

BY Michael B. slaughter

"There will be more rejoicing in heaven over one sinner who repents than over ninety-nine righteous persons who do not need to repent."
—Luke 15:7

Jesus' message connected best with those outside the institutional religious structures of his day. He crossed the taboo lines of gender and race by including women and samaritans in his message and ministry. He challenged the paradigms of religious correctness by his association with the spiritually unclean. Jesus endured the extreme rejection of the cross to reach those excluded by lifeless traditions, loveless law, and meaningless ritual.

People listened to Jesus because his message had authority (Luke 4:32). His words had a power that intersected vital issues of their daily experience. His words were profound yet simple, both comforting and afflicting. Jesus connected to the de-churched, using a spirit-empowered communication form that made ample use of image, metaphor, and storytelling.

At no other time in my ministry do I find a greater sense of joy than when preaching to a diverse group of people who are on the Jesus quest. However, preaching styles that communicated well to the seeker of the '80s are no longer the styles that best engage postmodern pilgrims. A whole new generation has grown up with no knowledge of or affinity toward the Bible, God's story. If we continue to preach using the models many of us learned in seminaries and Bible colleges during the last decades of the twentieth century, we'll remain essentially irrelevant to the de-churched people who God longs to reach.

Styles of effective preaching will be as varied and diverse as the uniqueness of each personality that God calls. No two preaching styles are the same, but all effective communicators understand their own unique gift mix as well as the unique culture to which they've been sent.

There are a few common denominators for preaching, however, that connect with persons who are outside of the church. Preaching that speaks to the heart of the de-churched person must be intentionally missional, multicultural, multisensory, and incorporate the postmodern language of multimedia.

> preaching styles that communicated well to the seeker of the '80s are no longer the styles that best engage postmodern pilgrims.

MISSIONAL

Jesus targeted a very specific audience. When others criticized him for hanging out with people of questionable business practices, he reminded his criticizers that "the Son of Man came to seek and to save what was lost" (Luke 19:10).

Jesus' mission focus was even more defined: "I was sent only to the lost sheep of Israel" (Matthew 15:24). "Lost" Jewish people were the target audience for Jesus' message. The poor and oppressed always received priority in his words and works. In his first known sermon at Nazareth, Jesus quoted from a passage in Isaiah: "The Spirit of the Lord is on me, because he has anointed me to preach good news to the poor" (Luke 4:18).

Jesus intentionally focused the scope of his message on a very specific group of people. These were the disenfranchised, those generally excluded from traditional religious practice and who represented a particular segment of the Palestinian culture.

Likewise, every effective communicator today will first clearly define the missional audience for the message and identify what that group of persons value. Who's your target audience?

The focus of my ministry is those who are tuned out or turned off by the traditional church. This is not to make a value statement on the traditional church or to attempt to measure the effectiveness of its mission. I'm simply called to connect with those folks who are not engaged by more traditional forms of Christianity. Church attendance in America has been on a steady decline. I want to reach those who are seeking an experience of God, yet question the relevance of the institutional church.

The people I best communicate with are those engaged by the art forms of pop culture. One of their favorite pastimes is channel surfing. They listen to rock, pop, country, and have had very little exposure to Christian music in any form. They see more movies than read books, yet they are well informed. They care about what's going on in the world around them and wrestle with issues related to marriage, divorce, parenting, work, and life meaning.

Seeking people are those who are truly asking God-questions. I'm not interested in trying to convince the unconvinced. The gospel of Jesus is radical and costly, and we must not back away from its demands.

One of the mistakes I made during the church-growth movement of the '90s was to overemphasize numbers of people attending worship as the measure of success. Size is not the measure of strength, however. It's not about how many are coming but about how loving are those who participate! How many are truly serving Christ's mission in their homes, workplaces, communities, and world?

> I want to reach those who are seeking an experience of god, yet question the relevance of the institutional church.

Jesus grew a congregation of only 120 by the end of his earthly ministry—not a very impressive number. He would have never been invited to speak at a church-growth conference! Yet he built those 120 kingdom servants into a movement whose influence would extend out to reach the world, eventually touching you and me.

I openly challenge seeking people to become real followers of Jesus Christ. Many of those who come "sampling" leave the church because it's not what they're looking for. Yet others stay and become deeply involved in a ministry of transformation, connecting with the hurting, poor, and disenfranchised people of the world.

My mission objective of connecting de-churched people engaged by the art forms of pop culture to radical discipleship has caused me to get back to the basics in my preaching themes. This past summer I preached a series on servanthood, which culminated in a commitment celebration where all participants signed their name to serve in one ministry area for one year (see Servant Catalog at www.Ginghamsburg.org/ministry/involve.htm).

I also taught a series on the Christian disciplines during the Lenten season. At the same time, our congregation began using a Transformation Journal, developed by our discipleship team, allowing us to read through the Bible together in a year (see Transformation Journal at www.Ginghamsburg.org/trans/readings.htm).

Service, cell group participation, and mission outreach are expected, not suggested. What does this imply? Some people are going to say, "It's too hard" and leave. I must confess—it hurts. Yet others will be transformed and will influence more people who will in turn influence even more for Jesus Christ.

> I'd rather preach to a church of 120 people who will impact the world than three thousand who are only inspired to live "a little better" lives.

I'd rather preach to a church of 120 people who will impact the world than three thousand who are only inspired to live "a little better" lives.

Who is your missional audience?

MULTI-CULTURAL

When I came to the little country church in the semirural-suburban community of Ginghamsburg twenty-some years ago, it was a homogeneous congregation. People essentially looked alike, thought alike, and voted alike. Diversity was limited to white- and blue-collar households. Everyone had names like Hugh, Peggy, Dennis, Mary, Frank, and Kathy.

The world has changed! I'm not preaching to the same culture that the bishop sent me to in 1979, even though I'm in the same geographical location. Today Yoon, Hisato, Chisa, Carmena, Jamaal, and Keigo are active participants in our fellowship. Asian, Hispanic, Anglo, and African Americans are all part of each weekend worship experience. They come from many different belief systems.

What's happening? A famous comedian said it best: "You know the world has turned upside down when the number one golfer is black and the number one rapper is white."

My children's generation is experiencing cultural crossover. Its taste in music includes R & B, rap, hip-hop, alternative, Latin, and country. And they had better be learning Spanish! Spanish is said to be the second language of the United States and its use is growing rapidly. At the same time, there has been a "mediazation" of global culture. The same movies, music, and fashion styles are embraced by a growing majority of cultures throughout the world. The homogeneous communities of the twentieth century are becoming the global villages of the twenty-first century.

The Japanese companies Honda and Panasonic are two of the largest companies in our area. Managers come from Japan for two- to four-year stints, become part of our neighborhood, and hopefully become part of our church. Most come from a Buddhist background with no real knowledge about Jesus. This too has changed my paradigm for preaching!

Preaching to the de-churched must be strategically multicultural and reflect the diversity of the geographic community—not the homogeneity of the typical local church. The effective twenty-first-century preacher will be intentionally multicultural. Two years ago I began subscribing to Ebony magazine. This has broadened my horizons and my illustration base from my accustomed weekly jaunts and journeys through Time and Newsweek. My wife and I make sure that we include non-Anglo movies in our entertainment mix. I regularly tune in to the BET network.

It's not enough to include multicultural references in my speaking. Our worship platform must also demonstrate ethnic and gender inclusivity. Who participates on the worship team and in the band will be observed by the postmodern, pre-Christian person who has come to expect diversity and inclusivity. Since I'm from an Anglo background, I make sure that a majority of our guest speakers are anointed persons of color. The images that we project on the screen also need to reflect the diversity of the de-churched community.

> preaching to the de-churched must be strategically multicultural and reflect the diversity of the geographic community.

Before people can hear our words, they must see our credibility. This is the miracle of Pentecost. On the day the Holy Spirit was given, people were gathered "from every nation under heaven" (Acts 2:5b). They spoke different languages and came from different cultures; but through the anointed, intentionally multicultural preaching of Peter, they came to faith in Jesus Christ.

Faithful churches of the twenty-first century will not be guided by the homogeneous church-growth principle of the '80s and '90s. They're authentic communities of faith that demonstrate Galatians 3:28: "There is neither Jew nor Greek, slave nor free, male nor female, for you are all one in Christ Jesus."

Does your preaching style reflect the diversity of the twenty-first-century global village?

Starbucks and Barnes & Noble sell more than coffee and books; they sell experience. These are places where people go to hang out. A customer can find a comfortable chair, peruse the latest issue of Real Simple, and sip a caramel latte. Why else would people pay three dollars for a specialty coffee when they can get a cup of coffee at the local gas station for less than a dollar? People are buying experience. Experience engages the whole person—sight, smell, hearing, touch, and taste. We're more than cerebral beings.

Modern preaching was essentially one-dimensional in that it was primarily a mental, logical, linear presentation. Postmodern seekers are not interested in an explanation about God. They are seeking an experience of God. William Hendricks, in his book *Exit Interviews: Revealing Stories of Why People Are Leaving the Church,* said that a major point of frustration was that the church did little to help people meet God.

Many successful models of ministry that attracted the baby boomer excelled in platform presentations that were targeted toward amassing crowds of spectators. Postmodern seekers are not seeking performance or entertainment. They want to experience the results of an encounter with the Divine and to participate in significant mission and purpose.

Multisensory preaching begins with the entire experience of the worship setting. The sensory experience of the worship environment plays a critical role in a person's receptivity to the Spirit and the spoken word. Is the environment warm, inviting, intimate, and personal, encouraging community while affirming the individual at the same time? Lighting, chair comfort, and alternative seating areas all affect a person's openness and receptivity. Is the setting cold or comfortable, institutional or warm? Is the facility accessible and user friendly? We offer cafe-style tables and chairs where people can sit and drink a specialty coffee, as well as padded chairs arranged in the more traditional-style rows.

> postmodern seekers are not interested in an explanation about god. They are seeking an experience of god.

Baby boomers responded to the mega-mall ministry complexes of the '80s and '90s, but twenty-first-century seekers prefer the intimacy of the "cafe." We recently decided not to build a three-thousand-seat sanctuary at Ginghamsburg. Large auditoriums tend to lose the sense of intimacy and community that smaller venues lend to the worship experience. Stadium-style seating promotes a sense of performance, not participation. We're going to continue to multiply worship experiences in smaller, more personal formats that promote both community and participation.

> Large auditoriums tend to lose the sense of intimacy and community that smaller venues lend to the worship experience.

Multisensory preaching is integrated within the whole worship experience. I couldn't begin to develop my message outside of a worship team. Kim Miller, our creative director, leads our worship team through each week's planning process. The group consists of a media director, graphic artist, music director, curriculum specialist, and preaching pastor. Curriculum is developed around the week's message for the cell groups (for more information, see www.Ginghamsburg.org/sermon/default.htm; also reference Bible Study format). The preaching and worship experience is then integrated into the overall discipleship strategy, allowing the messages to go beyond "head teaching" to whole-life integration.

Multisensory preaching engages the whole of a person's life experience. It goes beyond information to transformation. Most people are not living their God-wired dreams (see people's responses to "What is your wildest life dream?" at www.Ginghamsburg.org/dechurch/dream.htm). Preaching to the de-churched is about connecting the soul of each individual to his or her unique God-dream. Does your overall worship environment enhance or distract from the preaching experience?

MULTIMEDIA

The postmodern communicator must be fluent in the language of multimedia, connecting with those who speak it best. This generation has been saturated with media from the day they were born; from Mister Rogers to MTV; from the Gap to the "golden arches." The under-forty generations have been raised on an electronic playground. Atari, Nintendo, and Sega have been their babysitters; Sesame Street and MTV their tutors.

Our children have grown up in a world of visual imagery that defines their values, styles, vocabulary, and choices. The Internet allows endless visual travel without regulation, censor, or expense. This preoccupation with the screen has created a radical paradigm shift in the way things "make sense" to children, youth, and adults (see the book *Out on the Edge: A Wake-Up Call for Church Leaders on the Edge of the Media Reformation*). We have become increasingly visual and relate more quickly to pictures than to words. We are less attentive to lectures, which often lack motion, color, sound effects, visual effects, and music.

Jesus' messages were rich in visual images. "You are the salt of the earth (Matthew 5:13a). "You are the light of the world" (Matthew 5:14a). "A farmer went out to sow his seed" (Matthew 13:3b). "Suppose one of you has a hundred sheep and loses one of them?" (Luke 15:4a). "There was a man who had two sons" (Luke 15:11). "The kingdom of heaven is like a mustard seed" (Matthew 13:31a). Jesus understood that people are best engaged through pictures and story. "Jesus spoke all these things to the crowd in parables; he did not say anything to them without using a parable" (Matthew 13:34).

Many effective gospel communicators are using a diversity of media in their preaching. Everything from movie clips, video stories, personal interviews and graphic images to abbreviated dramas inserted within the context of the message. PowerPoint presentations of the '90s have paved the way for more sophisticated multimedia presentations that add depth and dimension to the spoken word.

Twenty-first-century moviegoers have been reintroduced to the wonderful storytelling of J.R.R. Tolkien through the visual art form of film. Many equally engaging film clips can make great insertion points in the context of a message. Ten years ago I would quote a line from a movie; now I show it. There are Web sites that speakers can refer to that connect illustrations from movies with a particular preaching theme. Check out these four Web sites:

- www.teachwithmovies.org

- www.textweek.com/movies/titleindex.htm

- www.hollywoodjesus.com

- www.imdb.com

> our children have grown up in a world of visual imagery that defines their values, styles, vocabulary, and choices.

Narrative storytelling is a renewed communication form of the twenty-first century. Video stories with engaging music beds are the mainstay of TV shows such as Oprah and Dr. Phil. These stories are also significant additions to nighttime TV news magazines. When done well, these pieces enhance the pace, rhythm, and emotional connection of the message.

> This preoccupation with the screen has created a radical paradigm shift in the way things "make sense" to children, youth, and adults.

I regularly use metaphors and video stories to illustrate my points. For example, "tent" is one of the metaphors I once used to illustrate the expansive nature that must characterize our "house of faith." "Enlarge the place of your tent, stretch your tent curtains wide, do not hold back; lengthen your cords, strengthen your stakes. For you will spread out to the right and to the left" (Isaiah 54:2-3a). We pitched a tent right on our platform that weekend! I cast the vision that we don't exist for ourselves but for the purpose of extending the love of Jesus Christ by bringing and including others. We exist for the purpose of the de-churched. Every Christian is called to do the work of an evangelist—no excuses.

I used a video story of a faithful, elderly servant in our fellowship to "visualize" this truth. Here's the slightly edited content of that video:

My name is Leland Sprecker. I'm ninety-four years old today, and I've been a Christian for eighty-six or eighty-seven years. I go to Ginghamsburg on Saturday nights.

If I sit down at the doughnut shop, if I don't know the person next to me, it doesn't take long before I strike up a conversation, asking, "Where do you go to church?"

"Well, I don't go."

That's a signal for me to go after 'em. I would say eighteen or twenty have been fetched in by my invitation. I always take them. I don't say, "You go and we'll meet you." I take one at a time usually. I enjoy seeing them, and I enjoy the service. I sort of feel good about doing that.

I find that at ninety-four I won't be around here much longer; I can't expect to. So I want to cover as much territory in this spiritual aspect as I can. We're told that that's one of the things we're to do is to be about His—capital H—business.

Long as I'm able, I'll be contacting individuals about their spiritual status. So I'll probably go on as long, long as I can (see the video at www.Ginghamsburg.org/dechurch/sprecker.htm).

The point is more effectively made with Leland's own words and expressions in the backdrop of his own home than I could ever make on my own through traditional oral communication. Folks are immediately engaged when the lights go down and the video comes up on the screen. The story engages the hearts, minds, and emotions of everyday people in the real world. "If a ninety-four-year-old can fetch them in, what's my excuse?" we find ourselves asking. Leland's story is a powerful testimony of a faithful disciple who's doing the work of an evangelist. You have "Lelands" in your church whose stories need to be told.

> folks are immediately engaged when the lights go down and the video comes up on the screen.

Stephanie Milas was born with a rare muscle disease that rendered her completely paralyzed. She's a beautiful, bright teenager who serves Christ's mission in an amazing, unusual way. Here's the slightly edited story, told through her mother, that I used to illustrate a message on servanthood:

My name is Carrie, and this is Stephanie, my daughter. When she was six months old, she was diagnosed with a muscular disease. We were told that if we were lucky, she would live to be two years old.

It was very hard for us to accept this. I thought my child may never walk, she may never do a lot of things that other kids will do, but even with all her adversities, her faith is so big and so large that she just blossoms. I am so proud to say, "Stephanie is my daughter."

When she was eight, she came to me one night and said, "Mom, I want to start saving pop tabs so I can help other kids." She had heard that a lot of times medical facilities would take pop tabs in exchange for therapies or radiation treatments, and she said, "Mom, people have done so much for me; I wanna give back." So I said, "OK, we'll start saving 'em." By word of mouth, Stephanie passed the word to all the people that she knows, and they began bringing pop tabs to us. The gallons just

PREACHING TO THE DECHURCH

came, and we had tabs coming from Arkansas and California. I would say she's collected a million and donated all of them.

We were at church a few weeks ago when they made an announcement of a little girl six years old that was in need of pop tabs to help pay for her leukemia treatments. That's when I thought, "I know where there's lots of pop tabs. This is where they're meant to go." Stephanie just smiled and said, "Mom, I'm so excited. When can we take 'em?"

I called them ahead of time and said, "Can someone meet me out front to help me unload these tabs?" They were like, "Yeah, sure." So when they met us out front they were like, "Oh my gosh; you do have some pop tabs!"

(See the video at www.Ginghamsburg.org/dechurch/milas.htm)

Stephanie donated fifteen gallons of pop tabs that afternoon. That collection alone took Stephanie more than one year to gather.

who in your faith community has a story that needs to be told?

Stephanie speaks in a small, nearly indecipherable voice: "It fills my heart with joy that I can help others the way they have helped me."

I just think it's wonderful that every time she hears that tab pop, she thinks of somebody else. I believe that we're all here for a purpose, and Stephanie's definitely sought out that purpose, and she's doing what she knows she can do to help someone else. My hopes are that when other people see what a difference she can make saving a few pop tabs, they'll do the same.

Stephanie's story engages the heart in a way that transcends my oral storytelling abilities. Who in your faith community has a story that needs to be told? Video stories about people of faith in your congregation have the potential to engage the hearts of those interacting with your message. Belief comes from the head; conviction comes from the heart.

How does the twenty-first-century communicator engage the mind and heart of the de-churched person? How do we proclaim and demonstrate the unchanging truth of the gospel?

- by communicating a well-articulated mission focus

- by demonstrating a commitment to being intentionally multi-cultural

• by integrating the preaching/messages into a wholistic, multi-sensory worship experience

• by translating the stories of God's grace through media, metaphor, and visual storytelling

...for there is rejoicing in heaven over one sinner who repents!

Michael B. Slaughter is the lead pastor and chief dreamer of Ginghamsburg Church, Tipp City, Ohio, and a catalyst for change in the worldwide church. His dynamic teaching, heart for the lost, and innovative approach to ministry have led Ginghamsburg Church to outgrow all paradigms for a church in a cornfield. He has published four books: *Spiritual Entrepreneurs* (Abingdon Press, October 1996); *Out on the Edge* (Abingdon Press, March 1998); *Real Followers: Beyond Virtual Christianity*, with Warren Bird (Abingdon Press, October 1999); and *unLearning Church*, with Warren Bird (Group Publishing, December 2001).

chapter fifteen

PREACHING ON MARRIAGE

BY BOB RUSSELL

I never used to speak on marriage. As a young preacher, I didn't have much personal experience in the matter, and I had grown up with parents who truly loved each other. I had no idea how stressful marriage was for many people.

As I began speaking about marriage, though, I discovered hurting people had been sitting in church for years, putting up a front, and wondering, "Is our marriage abnormal?" After a sermon on marriage, I'd hear, "It's so good to know we're not the only ones who struggle."

I concluded that most people want help with their marriage, even when they believe there's nothing more to do. So I decided to preach more intentionally about the subject.

THE CHALLENGES

As I did, I found that it's easy to preach about marriage but difficult to do it well. And it's getting more difficult.

One major challenge is how to make everyone in today's congregation feel included. Some have happy marriages, others have seen a divorce lawyer that week; some have been married three times, others have never married.

Another difficulty is how to illustrate the message. Stories carry emotional impact, and people in the congregation hold strong feelings about marriage—either their own, their parents' marriage, a failed marriage, or a marriage they wish they had.

A third challenge is how to talk about my own marriage without making myself look better or worse than I am and without invading my family's privacy.

Some preachers also wrestle with the need to preach about marriage when their own marriages are in trouble or when they're not married.

Here are some principles I've found helpful.

USE POSITIVE EXAMPLES WITHOUT GLAMORIZING

In a day when so many marriages break up, it's more important than ever to hold up successful marriages as examples. One idea, which I got from a friend, is when preaching on marriage to say occasionally, "I'd like for everybody who has been married for more than fifty years to stand." As they stand, I say, "These are heroes of our church." People burst into applause.

I tell of men and women who have stuck by their spouses. I told the story of Jim Irby, preacher at the church where I served as youth minister years ago. I saw him and his wife at a convention a while back. His wife, an elegant woman, now has a disease that has deteriorated her muscles until she can barely walk. As I saw this dignified couple in their late seventies walk into the room, Jim was walking at the same slow pace as his wife, bent in the same places she was bent, so he could hold on to her in support.

"That's what we all want," I said. "To have a companion who really believes what he or she said—'I'll stand by you in sickness and in health.' "

I also use strong examples of fidelity. When my friend Russ Blowers retired recently, somebody asked him, "What's the greatest accomplishment in your ministry?" He was president of our convention of Christian churches. His was one of the largest churches in Indianapolis. He headed the Billy Graham crusade there. Yet he didn't mention any of those things.

Russ said, "I'm most proud of the fact that I've never had to go into my children's bedroom and try to explain to them why I had been unfaithful to their mother."

On the other hand, it's possible to glamorize marriage too much. I've used a cartoon I found years ago of a beautiful girl driving an Italian sports car. The top is down on her convertible, she's smiling, her long hair is blowing in the breeze. There are two haggard, miserable-looking women, with babies on each arm, looking at her and saying, "Poor Nancy. She never could find a husband."

INCLUDE EVERYONE

When preaching about marriage, it's easy to make certain people feel excluded. I used to hear comments like "Why is it you never say anything about divorce?" or "How come you never preach to singles?" In recent years I haven't heard that as much because I now do two things.

■ **1. Listen to the experts.** I've never been through a divorce, but that doesn't mean I'm not authorized by God to preach on divorce. Since my experience is limited, though, I go to those who've experienced it. A few years ago, I preached a sermon on divorce and one on remarriage. To prepare, I gathered six or seven people who have wrestled with those issues firsthand, and said, "I've got some questions to ask you."

Later, when I preached, I said, "I've never been through a divorce, but I have some friends who have. Let me tell you what they said to me."

In addition, I scan periodicals geared for singles, divorced people, and single parents. There's an avalanche of information available on these issues. I have no excuse if I come across as ignorant.

Recently two women came to me and said, "We're part of a support group for women who are abused physically. Could you address this subject a little more in preaching?"

I was hesitant. The topic was so foreign to my experience. But two weeks ago, while talking about forgiveness and overcoming the pressures of the past, I said, "Maybe you have a husband who has beat you up." You could have heard a pin drop. After the service, a woman came to me and said, "I'm in an abusive situation right now. I don't know where to turn. Can you help me?"

■ **2. Include specific, one-line illustrations of various situations.** People need to know that I know they are present, and that the message is for them too.

It's easy to be generic in preaching: "Maybe you need to forgive somebody in your family." It may take me another fifteen minutes of thought to come up with a specific illustration: "Your dad ran out on you and your mom when you were six years old. When will you forgive him?"

By being more specific, I communicate: *I know you're out there. This sermon is for you, too.* Such one-line illustrations also communicate: *I recognize that your parents got a divorce. There are others here just like you, and you're welcome and accepted here.*

BALANCE HERO AND GOAT I try to balance illustrations in which I'm the hero or my family is ideal with illustrations that show me as the goat or that highlight my family in our day-to-day struggles.

Once I told about a time we were traveling on the East Coast and disagreed about whether I was driving in the right direction. Judy said, "You're going west."

I said, "I'm not either. I'm going east. We're going in the right direction." Each of us was convinced the other was wrong.

Then I saw a sign that she didn't see that told me I was going in the wrong direction. I drove past the next two exits trying to think of some way I could get off for gasoline and get back on without telling her I had changed directions.

> It's easy to be generic in preaching. It may take me another fifteen minutes of thought to come up with a specific illustration.

Often, it's harder for me to use an illustration that reveals the tenderness of our marriage. Several years ago, we went through a difficult period with Judy's health. That time of our lives was too tender to talk about for some time, but I finally got to the place where I could tell it without tearing up. One of the first times I made more than a passing reference to it was with this story:

When we celebrated our thirtieth wedding anniversary, I wanted to get Judy a ring that cost more than I felt I could afford. I'd always been a little embarrassed about the ring I gave her when we got engaged. Even after I took her engagement ring and the new ring to have the stones set, I kept debating whether I should have spent so much money. But just a few weeks later, when Judy lay in the hospital bed after a stroke, her left hand partially paralyzed, I looked down at her hand and said, "That sure is a pretty ring on your finger."

She replied, "I think it is too."

I wanted the story to remind people to demonstrate love before it's too late.

Sometimes, of course, a preacher may not be able to use personal illustrations because of marital struggles.

I have a preacher friend who has been holding on to his marriage with his fingertips for more than twenty years. He dreads preaching on marriage because he feels like a hypocrite. But he grits his teeth and looks for illustrations from the marriages of others. He might say, "My friend Bob Russell tells the story…" That technique may limit his effectiveness, but I respect him because he rises above his situation to preach on a subject that needs to be addressed.

BRING UP SEX—DISCREETLY

When anyone talks about problems, needs, and expectations in marriage, sex is always near the top of the list. I preach on the topic because I believe in preaching the whole counsel of God and because I want to speak to real life.

We encourage parents to put their kids in children's church, yet I'm more discreet about how I discuss sex than I was fifteen years ago. Back then I might have used the word *intercourse* in a sermon. Now I use the word *intimacy.* That may seem counterintuitive, given our exposure to the subject from pop culture. For example, fifteen years ago, many people recoiled at hearing the word *condom.* Few are shocked by it anymore. But it's because people get the full-frontal approach from television and movies that I want my approach to be tasteful.

I use personal illustrations on this topic only with caution, discretion, and permission. I've shared that one thing I love about Judy is that she's really affectionate. She's kind of formal in public, and it surprises some people that she would be that warm at home.

One night Judy and I were eating pizza with the youth after church in the church kitchen. Judy looked really pretty that night. She looked my way, and I winked at her. She looked away as if she was embarrassed, but later that night at home as I was sitting in my chair reading, she came up behind me, put her arms around my neck, and asked, "You know what it does to me when you wink at me like that in public?"

"No, not really."

Well, I found out, and I'm going to do it more often! A story like this has an important purpose: it signals to married people that it's OK to be affectionate, to desire your spouse, and to initiate intimacy.

POINT TO PRACTICAL HELP

I want a sermon on marriage to point people to the Source of hope. But many people need additional, practical assistance. Whenever possible, I point people to that.

In one message, I brought up the subject of being a single dad. I said, "Our society is becoming more sensitive to single moms; when you hear of single dads, it's usually deadbeat dads and dads who have abandoned their families.

"But statistically, fourteen out of one hundred custodial parents are fathers. Then there are dads who wish they could go back and relive their situations, but they can't. So if you're in that situation, there's a support group here that can help you."

BELIEVE IN THE POWER OF PREACHING

Despite the challenges, I keep preaching on marriage.

One couple, now married for more than twenty-five years, was in deep marital trouble about six years ago. They were not members of our church. They were separated, he had been running around on her, and a divorce was in the works. Somebody gave the wife a tape of one of my sermons on marriage, and she listened to it. When the husband came to pick up his things, he saw the tape on the counter and said, "What's this?"

She said, "It's by some preacher at Southeast Christian Church."

"Do you mind if I listen to it?"

"You can have it," she replied. "I'm finished with it." He headed to his apartment and started listening to the tape. He kept driving around until it was over. Then he drove back home and said to his wife, "I want to work on our marriage again."

They started coming to our church regularly, worked through their issues, and today are still together. They're so happy. They recently stopped me to introduce me to their daughter.

When I see God's Word turn around a marriage, that makes the hard work of preaching worthwhile.

This chapter is adapted from an article that originally appeared in LeadershipJournal © 1997 by Bob Russell. Used by permission.

At just twenty-two years of age, Bob became the pastor of Southeast Christian Church in Louisville, Kentucky. Thirty-five years later, that small congregation of 120 members has become one of the largest churches in America, with seventeen thousand people attending the three worship services every weekend. An accomplished author, Russell has written thirteen books, the latest titled *Jesus, Lord of Your Personality* (Howard Publishing, 2002). He also has a weekly column in The Lookout, a magazine printed by Standard Publishing. A highly respected speaker, Bob is heard weekly on *The Living Word*, a nationally syndicated radio program.

EVALUATION FOR
Great Preaching

Please help Group Publishing, Inc., continue to provide innovative and useful resources for ministry. Please take a moment to fill out this evaluation and mail or fax it to us. Thanks!

Group Publishing, Inc.
Attention: Product Development
P.O. Box 481
Loveland, CO 80539
Fax: (970) 292-4370

1. As a whole, this book has been (circle one)
   not very helpful   *very helpful*
   1   2   3   4   5   6   7   8   9   10

2. The best things about this book:

3. Ways this book could be improved:

4. Things I will change because of this book:

5. Other books I'd like to see Group publish in the future:

6. Would you be interested in field-testing future Group products and giving us your feedback? If so, please fill in the information below:

Name_____

Church Name _____

Denomination _____ Church Size _____

Church Address _____

City _____ State_____ ZIP _____

Church Phone _____

E-mail _____